The Historical Jesus and the Christ of Faith

The Historical Jesus and the Christ of Faith

Marcus Borg and N. T. Wright in Critical Dialogue

George Demetrion
Foreword by Glen Scorgie

WIPF *&* STOCK · Eugene, Oregon

THE HISTORICAL JESUS AND THE CHRIST OF FAITH
Marcus Borg and N. T. Wright in Critical Dialogue

Wipf & Stock
An Imprint of Wipf and Stock Publishers
199 W. 8th Ave., Suite 3
Eugene, OR 97401

www.wipfandstock.com

PAPERBACK ISBN: 978-1-5326-0328-0
HARDCOVER ISBN: 978-1-5326-0330-3
EBOOK ISBN: 978-1-5326-0329-7

Manufactured in the U.S.A.   DECEMBER 20, 2016

Dedication

I dedicate this book to you, Sue, my most beautiful wife, for your love, support, understanding, and for the life we have shared these past thirty-eight years. It is an understatement to say that this project would not have been undertaken without your support. For you have given me the space to live the life to which I feel called, in which I hope I have provided similar space for you. I continue to appreciate our daily reading of Scripture, devotional books, and studies by such authors as John Piper, C. S. Lewis, R. C. Sproul, Charles Stanley, Dallas Willard, and others that keep us both grounded in prayer, meditation, theologically-based spirituality, and the presence of God's Spirit, without which, any work that I might undertake in biblical and theological studies would be utterly meaningless. This devotional time provides the foundation for everything we do and everything we are. Thank you for being my life partner. We have been graced by much through these past decades in our life together in Hartford, Syracuse, and San Diego.

Contents

Foreword

JESUS IS *THE* TOWERING figure in the history of humanity. Even the giants among us must line up somewhere behind him. Allegiance to him is the defining feature of the Christian faith experience. And Jesus's identity remains—as indeed it has been from the very beginning—paramount in Christianity's engagement with the world's other great religions and secular worldviews. The question Jesus once posed to his band of followers still asks for response: Who do you say that I am?

Almost everything known or assumed about Jesus of Nazareth is found in the four Gospel narratives, located at the front of the canonical New Testament. These Gospels are tantalizingly brief portraits—each skillfully depicting Jesus from a particular authorial perspective and with a particular authorial agenda. Classic Christianity has assumed that these four portraits were so superintended by the Holy Spirit in their composition as also to constitute the very words of God. And classic Christianity inferred from this claim of divine authorship (or, more precisely, divine co-authorship) that the portraits mirror the perfect truthfulness of God's own character and word.

As long as such assumptions about the verbal inspiration of the four Gospels prevailed, the Christian answer to the question of Jesus's identity was straightforward: simply take the Gospel portraits at their face value. In recent centuries, however, at least a couple of developments have unsettled the composure of the faithful in their perceptions of the real Jesus. One has been the widening gap between the wonder-world of the Gospel narratives (filled as they are with divine-human communication and staggering supernatural events) and the modern worldview with its profound skepticism about any suggestion that the natural laws of the physical universe can be, or ever were, suspended. As a result, modern readers of the Gospels often experience enormous cognitive dissonance. Many events recorded in the Gospels exceed what their sincere but thoroughly modern mindsets can plausibly entertain.

A second challenge to classic Christianity's unencumbered embrace of Jesus as portrayed in the Gospels has also emerged. It surfaced as scholars took a harder look at reconciling the New Testament portraits of Jesus into a single, synthesized account. So many things didn't appear to add up—didn't perfectly fit together—that questions surfaced about the Gospel authors' absolute commitment to factual reporting. Perhaps the Gospel writers thought of themselves as working in a different genre of literature, one that allowed for a degree of stylizing in their writing practices. Perhaps, then, the fault lies not with the original writers, but with contemporary readers who try to impose upon the Gospels a standard of objective, photographic-like reporting that is actually alien to the original authors' intentions.

The history of Christian mission and evangelization offers convincing proof that the Jesus proclaimed in the Gospels has the power to win worshipful allegiance, to transform lives, to give hope in the face of death, and to inspire all manner of good works. This *kerygamatic* Jesus—the Christ of apostolic proclamation and classic Christian faith—changes individual lives and sometimes whole societies.

But the question persists: To what extent is this Savior a pious fiction, an imaginary figure disconnected from earthy, ordinary reality? In the end, how is the Christ of classic faith any different, ontologically, from a movie character, a Disney creation or a Marvel comics super-hero?

Persons of integrity find it impossible to perpetuate the myth of Jesus Christ purely for its therapeutic effects. All Christian virtues are grounded in a prior and antecedent love for truth, and a vision of truth as that which corresponds to reality. It requires submission to what *is*. The Christian faith is not grounded solely in noble ideals, but also in the conviction that certain things actually happened. In no sphere is this truer than in the domain of Christology.

George Demetrion has done us a great service. He invites us into his own informed exploration of this perennial question of the truth about Jesus. His strategy is both humble and informed. He joins a stimulating conversation between two accomplished New Testament scholars as they wrestle with the question of the degree to which the Gospel accounts of Jesus correspond to historic reality. Marcus Borg and N. T. Wright are world-class scholars at opposing ends of a spectrum of conviction, and George weighs the arguments of each in an insightful yet respectful way. In the end, we discover where George personally lands. But more importantly, we are able to join him in his journey so that we can find the way to our own answers.

We live in an age of trivialization and distraction, one that grows quickly impatient with protracted arguments and scholarly details. But the questions engaged in this little book are far from trivial, and warrant our close reading.

In *Higher Superstition* (1994), Paul Gross and Norman Levitt have written: "Science succeeds precisely because it has accepted a bargain in which even the boldest imagination stands hostage to reality. Reality is the unrelenting angel with whom scientists have agreed to wrestle."[1] So, like George Demetrion, must all honorable Christians as well.

Glen G. Scorgie
Professor of Theology and Ethics
Bethel Seminary San Diego

---

1. Quoted by Jeeves, *Human Nature at the Millennium*, 144.

Preface

LIKE MANY OTHER WORKS, this project has been long in the making. I originally intended this study as one of two introductory chapters in my recent book, *In Quest of a Vital Protestant Center*. In my planning model, these chapters were designed to highlight what I refer to as the great divide between modernism and fundamentalism on the role of the Bible in relation to the culture that undergirds virtually all aspects of twentieth- and twenty-first-century U.S. Protestant theology and religious culture. This fissure would need to be worked through as part of the essential work for discriminating evangelicals and postliberal theologians and biblical scholars to establish more mediating frames of reference without minimizing areas of persisting disagreement. For this effort, I built on the work of Phillips and Okholm in *The Nature of Confession: Postliberals and Evangelicals in Conversation*, as well as various texts by Gabriel Fackre, as summarized in the title of one of his more influential books, *Ecumenical Faith in Evangelical Perspective*.

In its initial chapter format, as well as in its current short monograph design, I sought through the essay review format of Marcus Borg's and N. T. Wright's, *The Meaning of Jesus*, to highlight the divides in current Protestant discourse between what is commonly referred to as the historical Jesus and the Christ of faith. As I was formulating the structure of *In Quest of a Vital Protestant Center*, I intended that chapter to serve as a contemporary correlative to the book's current historically-focused second chapter that tracks the tensions within the great divide through three pivotal time periods throughout the twentieth century. In the end, I reasoned that two introductory chapters of this sort represented too complex of a dialectic for the more constructive work that comprised the main focus of *In Quest of a Vital Protestant Center*.

This current book examines the sharp differences between the Jesus Seminar perspective of Borg, who emphasizes the discontinuities between the life and times of Jesus of Nazareth and the Christ of faith, with the more clearly equivocal, theological traditionalist, Wright, who draws out the continuities. Throughout the descriptive first four chapters, I focus on the ways in which Borg and Wright diverge on a variety of critical issues. I concentrate on sources of evidence upon which each author stakes out his argument, their opposing views on the messianic claims of Jesus of Nazareth, and Christological issues, particularly on the incarnation and the atonement, the latter of which Borg places in the category of a historical accident. In the process, I highlight my disagreements with Borg, whose vision of Jesus, while rooted in first-century Jewish religious thought and the gospels narratives, finds its ultimate meaning in a more universal religious vision that transcends the radical particularity of any given tradition.

I find persuasive much of Wright's argument pointing to greater continuity between the Jesus depicted in the gospels and the life and times of Jesus of Nazareth, including an appreciation of the extensive evidence he amasses in arguing for the historical validity of the post-resurrection sightings. For Wright, the ultimate significance of Jesus and the basic meaning structure of the Christian faith reside within the core claims of the gospel itself, as well as the entire New Testament, when his specialized studies and popular books and New Testament study guides are looked at together as a unified body of work. For him, these claims gain a great deal of credibility through their substantial congruity, as far as can be determined, with the historical record.

My concern is that Wright relies too much on history in linking the claims of the gospels, as well as the letters of Paul, to the actual events surrounding the life and ministry of the historical Jesus. It is one thing to argue, as he does, that the gospel writers believed that what they reported actually took place as written. It is also one thing to argue, as Wright does, that the historical events surrounding the life and times of Jesus of Nazareth are central to the faith in the risen Christ that emerged in early Christianity. It is another matter, altogether, to claim that we can have knowledge of those events to a high degree of certitude, especially of the post-crucifixion events. While Wright notes the distinction, in appropriating a critical realist historical methodology to his analysis of the evidence, he downplays the significance of the potential gaps between the claims and the realities of what actually happened in a specific time and place, to the extent that the latter can be ever be discerned.

That there was a correlation of some profound sort seems almost tautological. Yet, whatever historical knowledge emerges in the study of the life and times of Jesus of Nazareth, the primary source remains the New Testament, a specific Christological text that, in terms of historical illumination, is both revealing and veiled. With Wright, I find much value in interpreting the life and ministry of Jesus through the similarities and dissimilarities of Second Temple Judaism, particularly in its first century manifestations. This is a central focus of Wright's magnificent *Jesus and the Victory of God*. Nonetheless, much remains beyond definitive historical disclosure, especially concerning the consciousness of Jesus and the post-crucifixion events. While the life, ministry, and crucifixion of Jesus in its relation to the faith in the resurrected Christ, as it emerged initially in the decade of the 30s, is connected in some ineradicable way, the manner of its occurrence remains the critical issue.

As depicted in the scholarship over the past two centuries, it is not beyond the realm of reasonable conjecture that there may be more discontinuity between the events as portrayed in the gospels and what actually transpired in real time and place than Wright envisions. At the least, this is a contestable matter. To the extent that there is more discontinuity than Wright acknowledges, this would require him to expand his interpretative reach beyond his emphasis on the continuities, particularly when the post-Pauline epistles and the Gospel of John are factored in. This would call for some rethinking about the role of history in its relation to faith, particularly on the relationship between Jesus as the Jewish Messiah, as Wright interprets it, and the incarnate Christ begotten as the very Word of God, both of which are highlighted with varying degrees of emphasis when the entirety of the NT canon is taken into account.

Borg opens up such a prospect of exploring the discontinuities. However, he does so only by a metaphorical interpretation of the risen Christ in finding its meaning in a more universal depiction of the holy that transcends the specific language claims of the New Testament. With Wright, I find the textual claims of the New Testament canon, taken as a whole, central to the vital proclamation of an authentic Christian faith, which I cannot separate from the Great Tradition of Christian orthodoxy. While the Christian revelation has taken place in and through history, it also transcends history in its ultimate orientation in an incarnational and Trinitarian God that can be drawn out of the New Testament, as processed through the ecumenical multi-century orthodox Christian tradition. Wright embraces this view, especially in his more popular books, where he brings together his role as a historian and his pastoral calling as an Anglican bishop.[1]

In even partially working through the continuity/discontinuity issue, there are a variety of critical factors to take into account. One is that the period immediately following the post-crucifixion events remain largely opaque to exacting historical analysis, which is an enduring sticking point underlying all research on the Jesus of history. The positions of Wright and Borg are invariably rooted in the presuppositions that give shape to the specific inferences and conjectures they make. Regardless of the stances they take on the relationship between the life and times of Jesus of Nazareth and the rise of the Christian faith in the risen savior, their respective conjectures extend beyond the evidence needed to adequately support them.

Another consideration is the highly likely prospect, based on the evidence presented by Paul (1 Cor 15:3–8), that the crucifixion,

---

1. Wright, *Simply Christian*, 138–40.

burial, and resurrection sightings, together, were part and parcel of the earliest post-crucifixion foundational set of beliefs, rather than a product of a developing church tradition, which is not to deny later gospel accretions. How and why that early Christian vision emerged remains, in many ways, unclear. That it took place within history is a given, a topic, itself, worthy of much historical analysis, as Wright notes.[2] Nonetheless, given the very nature of the proclamation of the risen Christ, it is, in the language of faith, an enduring mystery that, while breaking forth in and through history, has a transcendent dimension that cannot be fully explained or grasped through historical analysis.

From a faith perspective, I can only assume that some profound occurrence between what is commonly referred to as supernatural and natural causes were at work, which I link to an underlying hermeneutical stance "that God . . . in Christ [is] reconciling the world to himself " (2 Cor 5:19, NKJV). In this, I posit that the very mediation of the Jesus of history and the Christ of faith took place in a realm of what the Christian historian Gary Dorrien depicts as "true myth," what C. S. Lewis portrays as the mysterious merger of fact and myth, what Hans Frei identifies as a storied narrative, and what J. I. Packer refers to as a mystery. However different the perspectives of these authors may be in their nuanced relationship between faith and history, they share a common belief that God, in fact, acted in and through the historical Jesus in a manner that has ontological standing in the real world of actual existence. To a person, these authors insist that there is more than *merely* the mythical in their various depictions of the risen Christ of faith, without reducing one iota the mystery of revelation. In this they share the perspective of the New Testament writers in viewing the risen Christ through the prism of a believing faith community, without which one would remain without spiritual sight (Luke 24:24–30, John 20:24–29, Heb 11:6).

By linking what those earliest followers of Jesus believed to what is stated in the synoptic gospels as closely approximating what actually happened, Wright places his interpretation firmly

---

2. Wright, *Contemporary Quest for Jesus*, 68–87.

within what he refers to as the third quest for the historical Jesus, one situated within the apocalyptic setting of Second Temple Judaism. In his interpretation, Jesus' messianic identity was thoroughly rooted in the post-exilic vision of the greater-than-David Davidic "king through whose work YHWH was at last restoring his people."[3] Wright notes that this is a good distance from any acknowledgement that Jesus envisioned himself as the savior of the world or had any foreknowledge that his death was related to the propitiation of sin through the shedding of his blood (Rom 3:25). He also rejects any notion that Jesus of Nazareth viewed himself as the incarnation of God in human flesh or as the Second Person of the Trinity, as discerned through the Johannine prologue and John 17, or had any notion of himself as "the image of the invisible God, the firstborn over all creation" (Col 1:15). Nonetheless, as Wright understands it, as the climax of the covenant, Jesus fulfills Israel's destiny of restoring the world to a right relationship to the living God by becoming a light onto the Gentiles.

He acknowledges that "the attempt to move from Jesus to Christology," which the Christian faith demands, "calls for further reflection"[4] that, for him, requires pushing history and faith as far as he can and working through the dialectic that invariably bursts forth through such an encounter. I seek to engage in a similar dynamic, but one that places the priority on faith, revealed, first and foremost, in and through, the canonical Scripture, drawing on history for further illumination. To put a twist on Wright's depiction, this is a move from Christology to Jesus, which draws on history for supportive insight, in which *Jesus and the Victory of God* is one most valuable resource.

Regardless of whether one accepts the "collapse of history" in contemporary biblical hermeneutics, as some have posited,[5] there is an emphasis, particularly in postliberal biblical interpretation,

---

3. Wright, *Christian Origins and the Question of God,* 2:477. For the greater than Davidic reference, see Wright's discussion on Jesus' appropriation of Psalm 110. Ibid., 508–10.

4. Wright, *Contemporary Quest for Jesus,* 87.

5. Perdue, *Collapse of History.*

on two interweaving strands leading to a post-critical reading of Scripture. One is the impetus in narrative theology of interpreting the Bible as a realistic-like text "that is often 'history-like' even when it is not likely history."[6] The closely related other is that such an interpretation opens up an imaginative pathway of appropriating the Barthian dictum of reading the world through the prism of the revealed Word.[7] Envisioning the Bible through such a mode opens up a way of working through the literature on the various quests for the historical Jesus, in part, by bypassing the fact/fiction dilemma that underlay the quest. This allows the Bible to speak in and through its own unique idioms in its depiction of Jesus Christ in a manner that can incorporate the synoptic narratives with the gospel of John and the highest of the Christological epistles in a complexly unified vision of the Word made flesh.

It is not that the historical questions about the life and times of Jesus of Nazareth, including the post-crucifixion sightings, are unimportant; they most assuredly are, but they are not "determinative."[8] In part, that is because they are inconclusive, as the evidence stands. If one assumes that the disclosure of the Word-become-flesh is a given for the faith community, in no small measure, through a canonical-spanning revelation of the inscripturated NT canon, the specific biblical genres through which that understanding emerges (including the historical) are less important than the revelation itself. Viewed in this way, knowledge of the various genres upon which the canon is comprised provides invaluable insight in better understanding the dynamics of biblical revelation, but are not determinative of it.

No doubt, a radical gap between the person portrayed in the totality of the biblical image of Jesus Christ and the person who actually lived and died in real time and place would present a

---

6. Lindbeck, *Nature of Doctrine*, 122.

7. The classic postliberal texts are Frei, *Eclipse of Biblical Narrative* and Lindbeck, *Nature of Doctrine*, in which both authors acknowledge their debt to Barth. Both of these works underlie Purdue's *Collapse of History* and Dorrien's *Word as True Myth*, which I draw on in the concluding section of the book.

8. Lindbeck, *Nature of Doctrine*, 120.

theological crisis of no minor proportions. History matters. Whatever limitations there may be in the third quest for the historical Jesus, the messianic figure portrayed in *Jesus and the Victory of God* provides sufficient basis for an embrace of the high Christology that characterizes John and some of the epistles when the entirety of the New Testament is taken into account. Through such a comprehensive embrace of the NT canon, I seek to complement Wright's study by building bridges between postliberal and evangelical biblical scholars and theologians on the nature of revelation of God in Christ reconciling the world and to search out its historical roots. By the very nature of the search, any such attainment can only be highly partial; it represents an area of research that would require much discerning acuity, well beyond what I can explore here. Putting such caveats aside, I posit that a fourth quest would start with the Christ revealed throughout the New Testament as the starting point for looking to history in search of vital points of connection to the living past. This would call for a different set of hypotheses than those laid out by Wright in his critical realist historical methodology, ones that would complement his, while directing the ongoing research project in some new directions.

Acknowledgments

I AM GRATEFUL THAT at Bethel Seminary in San Diego, I had the opportunity to audit the fall 2015 seminar, "Exploring Continuity and Discontinuity between Early Christianity and Formative Judaism," offered by Donald Hagner, George Ladd Professor Emeritus Professor of New Testament at Fuller Theological Seminary. The course required a close reading of two important books by New Testament scholar, Richard B. Hays, *Echoes of Scripture in the Letters of Paul* and *Reading Backwards: Figural Theology and the Fourfold Gospel Witness*. As a result of the course I gained a deeper appreciation of the many Old Testament echoes that were on the surface or could be teased out in a wide range of New Testament passages and the importance of a figural reading in understanding the relationship of the two testaments. Through further research, I became aware of the close association between the scholarship of Hays and N. T. Wright. As a way of following up on the work of Hays and Wright, Don's seminar gave me the impetus to complete *The Historical Jesus and the Christ of Faith*.

I am especially indebted to Bethel Seminary Professor of Theology and Ethics, Glen Scorgie for the detailed attention he has generously given to this project. In an initial review of the book, Glen encouraged me to strengthen the concluding chapter. I'm not sure I met all of his concerns, but the result is that I concentrated a great deal on sharpening my concluding remarks. Glen's more recent commentary on this project is reflected in the Foreword. Through his own interpretive lens on the critical issues confronting contemporary believers in coming to terms with the truth claims of the Christian revelation in light of the powerful challenges of science, history, and literary studies, Glen aptly draws out the subtext of my book. I am honored that Glen has lent such energy and time to this book.

In addition, I have gained much by auditing several courses that Glen taught at Bethel Seminary. His seminar titled, "History of Christian Thought: 19th Century to the Present," was most germane to this current project. The assigned text, Roger Olson's, *The Journey of Modern Theology: From Reconstruction to Deconstruction*, provided the most comprehensive overview of the past two centuries of Western theology that I had ever encountered. Through Glen's lectures, seminar discussions, and Olson's text—which I supplemented with Gary Dorrien's indispensable, *Word as True Myth: Interpreting Modern Theology*—I greatly increased my understanding of the history underlying the various quests for the historical Jesus so pervasive throughout the nineteenth and twentieth centuries. As a result of the seminar, I also took a close look at Stanley Grenz's postconservative evangelical theology, which filled an important gap in my knowledge.

I learned a good deal, as well, from Glen's other courses. His seminar on the theology of the atonement significantly expanded my understanding of this topic and opened me up to the rich diversity and range of evangelical theology, of which I was largely unaware. His course on the pietistic tradition, of which I had limited knowledge, supplemented my appreciation of Puritan spirituality. The result is that I now have a deeper awareness of how these two central streams of Protestant devotional literature converge, and in places, diverge. Here is gist for additional work that continues to pull on me. What I appreciate, as well, is Glen's capacity to blend rigorous theological analysis with his deep sense of Christian spirituality, which is very much in keeping with the mission, vision, and values of Bethel Seminary. I also appreciate Glen's dedication to the theological and spiritual development of his students, to which he is most solicitous. I, for one (an auditor), have been very enriched by his attentive consideration of my theological and spiritual development.

I am grateful to the pastoral and staff team and the excellent lay leaders at College Avenue Baptist Church in San Diego for the spiritual nurturance that my wife and I gleaned through worship, the preached word, and small group study. What we found at CAB were individuals across the congregation with deep biblical faith, high character and integrity, and a searching quest for a penetrating understanding of the faith in all dimensions characteristic of Christian adult education at its very best. The Bethel and CAB experience, together, have made a permanent mark on my own Christian formation, for which I remain forever thankful.

I am also grateful for the unique niche of Wipf & Stock publishers for making available studies like this that seek to probe into critical theological topics that, for a variety of reasons, would have a hard time gaining traction in more traditional Christian publishing markets. In looking at the range and depth of texts that Wipf & Stock has made available over the years, in their countercultural publishing orientation, they are helping to redefine the realm of legitimacy in the academic Christian publishing sector. Brian Palmer, Editorial Administrative Assistant, Matthew Wimer, Assistant Managing Editor, Matthew Perkins, and Joshua Little, my copy editors, and Ben Dieter, Digital Content Editor, have been most helpful. I am grateful, as well to my sister-in-law, Audrey Lapointe for closely editing portions of this book. Audrey has a keen eye for the nuances of grammatical detail and word choice, which has been quite helpful.

George Demetrion
September 26, 2016
East Hartford, CT

Abbreviations

ESV English Standard Version
KJV King James Version
NKJV New King James Version

Unless otherwise indicated, all biblical references are from the (NIV) New International Version.

To discern God's purpose and to be obedient to it among all the ambiguities and perplexities of life is always a struggle. We may be often wrong both in our understanding of what God is doing in our attempted obedience, just as it is made clear in Scripture that the people whose stories it tells were often wrong, or only partially right, in their discernment of God's purpose. At best, we can hope to choose the relatively better and to reject the relatively worse. We can never claim that either our understanding or our action is completely right. That kind of proof belongs only to the end. As part of the community that shares in the struggle, we open ourselves continually to Scripture, always in company with our fellow disciples of this and former ages and in the context of the struggle for obedience; and we constantly find in it fresh insights into the character and the purpose of the one who is "rendered" for us in its pages. We read these pages, naturally, as part of our real history, secular history, the history of which we are a part. What other history is there? There are not different histories, but there are different ways of understanding history. We recognize this because another way of understanding history is being applied to contemporary events around us all the time. It is possible, and in our culture normal, to exclude the name of God altogether from our account of public affairs, and to construe history as a continuum of cause and effect, an area where 'historical forces' are at work and events take place in accordance with the only purposes at work are those of individual human beings.

But it is idle to suppose that any kind of peaceful coexistence is possible between these two ways of understanding history. It is clearly an illusion to imagine that there are two kinds of history—sacred and profane, salvation history and secular history. We who are at the moment making and suffering history know that there is only one history, but we know that it can be understood theistically or atheistically. It is true that a methodological atheism may be required in the course of historical study, just as a scientist may eliminate any concern with the music while he studies the movement of the pianist's fingers. But those who belong to the community that is controlled by the rendering of God in Scripture will surely be precluded from a dichotomizing of their lives into a private sphere where God is acknowledged and a public sphere in which events are finally interpreted without reference to God. The long-running debate about the relationship between the Jesus of history and the Christ of faith is simply one manifestation of the illusion that has haunted our culture ever since the Enlightenment. There is only one Jesus and one history. The question is whether the faith that finds its focus in Jesus is the faith with which we seek to understand the whole of history, or whether we limit this faith to a private world of religion and hand over the public history of the world to other principles of explanation.

—NEWBIGIN, *FOOLISHNESS TO THE GREEKS*, 60–61.

1

Overview

THE WIDELY READ *The Meaning of Jesus: Two Visions*, co-authored by Marcus Borg and N. T. Wright, provides an excellent entry point for probing critical issues in contemporary Protestant thought and religious culture. Borg was one of the members of the Jesus Seminar and Distinguished Professor in Religion and Culture at Oregon State University. His two books, *Meeting Jesus Again for the First Time* and *Reading the Bible Again for the First Time*, have provided many mainline clergy and theologically astute lay persons a way of reconciling their understanding of modern reality with the ancient and timeless truths of the Christian revelation without the need to take the Bible literally, or as synonymous with actual historical fact. Wright is currently Research Professor of New Testament and Early Christianity at the University of Saint Andrews in Scotland and former Anglican Bishop of Durham. He is one of the major authors of the "New Paul" school of biblical interpretation.

The alternative perspectives of these highly influential Christian authors, whose cumulative work spans a wide range of scholarly and more popular church-based discourse communities, crystallize key theological disputes between liberal Protestant and evangelical theology, particularly on the relationship between what is commonly dubbed as the "historical Jesus" and "the Christ of faith." The back cover of the book hypes the contrast between the liberal and "traditional" credentials of Borg and Wright respectively, a point well taken, yet with advisement in that, as a major proponent of the "New Paul" scholarship, some of Wright's claims have raised major concerns among traditional evangelicals over the role of the atonement and the central Reformation doctrine of justification by faith.[1]

The contrast is clear enough in that Borg points to the many retrojections of key Old Testament passages and allusions by the early church in the New Testament that the biblical writers drew upon to highlight the Christological significance of the Risen One, depicted as the "son of God." Borg notes that the New Testament contains deified depictions of Jesus, which, according to the proponents of the Jesus Seminar, are beyond any self reference to the historical personage of what Jesus of Nazareth would have likely said about himself.[2]

In faith, Borg accepts the Christological claims of God indwelling in Christ and discovers both Jesus and the Bible anew. However, it is a depiction which is metaphorical—the way in which God speaks to a specific faith community in and through its own particular idiom. This keeps open the possibility—and on Borg's reading—the likelihood that God speaks as fully to other

---

1. There is a great deal of pro and con material available on the New Paul literature. For a representative critique see Piper, *Future of Justification*. I bypass a discussion of the New Paul literature because (a) this essay is focused on interpretations of Jesus rather than Paul; (b) in contrast to Borg, Wright does argue for a more traditional, biblically-based interpretation, even as it is one that places a great deal of weight on history as lived by the Jewish Jesus as sifted through the "third quest" for the historical Jesus literature. In *Contemporary Quest for Jesus*, Wright provides a useful overview of the research on the historical Jesus, extending back to the nineteenth century.

2. Borg rejects "a sharp either-or choice between" (*Meaning of Jesus*, 252) the historical Jesus and the Jesus portrayed in the gospels as the sole arbiter of significance, maintaining that his faith has been shaped in a reflection on their interaction. Nonetheless, in contrast to Wright, Borg posits a radical distinction between the historical personage of Jesus of Nazareth and the portrayed Christ of the New Testament.

faith communities in other ways. The claim of the radical particularity of Christ as the full embodiment of God in human flesh is categorically rejected by Borg, even as such imagery speaks profoundly to the believing faith community. In his primary focus on the existential significance of Christ's mediation of God in the light of the compelling epistemological challenges of the contemporary era and the ongoing work of constructing the historical record, the question of ultimate truth remains largely unexamined in Borg's depiction of Jesus.

Building on the work of E. P. Sanders, J. D. Dunn, and others in reconstructing the "Jewish Jesus," Wright places the mission of Jesus within the historical context of Second Temple Judaism. From such a vantage point, this makes plausible the view that Jesus self-understood his calling as Israel's Messiah, which was not simply a later retrojection by the early church. Notwithstanding this grounding in Israel's history, the Messiah, as embodied by Jesus, radically reconstructed prevailing perceptions of a liberating king in the image of a conquering David. This somewhat altered perception of God on a cross could find justification in Jewish scripture as a plausible hypothesis retrospectively, once the vision was unleashed of Christ as crucified *and* resurrected redeemer king. In this respect, Wright takes on the challenge of historical Jesus scholarship and gives it a new twist in drawing out what he views as the ample ground of considerable continuity between the Jesus of history and the Christ of faith, as expressed particularly in the synoptic gospels and the letters of Paul. In his various work, Wright presents a plausible depiction of Jesus' self-understanding based on this reconstructed messianic vision, thoroughly congruent with the deepest teachings of Israel's God as suffering servant.[3]

The lurking concern remains the place of historical accuracy as the basis for faith. From the perspective of narrative theology, establishing greater linkages between history and the biblical text

---

3. For Wright's most extensive statement of this thesis, see *Christian Origins and the Question of God*, 2, titled *Jesus and the Victory of God*, which includes an important one hundred page overview of the scholarly literature, through what he describes as the "third quest" for the historical Jesus. That overview is repeated in a short, separate volume, *Contemporary Quest for Jesus*.

enhances credibility, if only in the respect that if an utterly radical disconnect between the historical Jesus and the Christ of faith existed, credulity would, at the least, be severely strained. That is, narrative theology works—to the extent that it does—because there is an inextricable (though far from thoroughly explainable) analogue between that which is depicted in the text and that which actually existed, as far as the historical record can disclose.[4]

In the very process of establishing a tighter connection between faith claims and the historical record, a concern arises that Wright places too much emphasis on historical accuracy as the basis for a faith stance that needs to remain grounded in "the substance of thing hoped for, the evidence of things not seen" (Heb 11:1, KJV). With Wright, I recognize the significance of the historical events surrounding the life and mission of Jesus of Nazareth for an incarnational faith, which is not synonymous with necessarily

---

4. This leaves open the matter on whether the viability of scriptural revelation depends on the historical accuracy of the text, in contrast to the genre of a realistic narrative, which incorporates both historical and fictive elements, an issue that goes to the heart of the difference between traditional evangelical and postliberal narrative biblical theologies (Phillips and Okholm, *Nature of Confession*). While the Bible includes a variety of genres in addition to the narrative mode, in the broadest of strokes, the Christian story, to use Fackre's designation, is rooted in the grand narrative that extends from creation to consummation, in which each biblical "chapter" delineates an essential component of the story. In his view of narrative theology—which incorporates both evangelical and postliberal perspectives—"the Bible is a book that tells [in the language of postliberal theologian, George Lindbeck] an 'overarching story.'" Fackre, *Doctrine of Revelation*, 3. More specifically, the Bible unfolds through a plotline that incorporates "the imaginative role of the narrator in telling the tale [that] does not preclude the historical core of the account" (20). Through this "Great Narrative [italics removed] within Scripture" (6) the primary source of the revelation of God in Christ is "traced by canonical hand" (3). In referring to the Bible as the primary *source* of revelation, Fackre identifies "Jesus Christ," himself, as "the interpretive key to the whole narrative" (5), in which the source and the very essence of revelation can be grasped, only in their interaction. Such interplay includes the *illumination* of the Holy Spirit in the mind and spirit of the writers and readers of the biblical narrative through which the mystery of God in Christ reconciling the world is disclosed. For a broader discussion of the biblical trajectory of Fackre's narrative theology, see *Christian Story*, 1 and *Doctrine of Revelation*. For an interpretive overview of Fackre's theology, see Demetrion, *In Quest of a Vital Protestant Center*, 115–66.

accepting the historical accuracy of the descriptive New Testament narratives of the events surrounding the empty tomb and resurrection sightings. A surer basis—one grounded in faith, as discussed in some depth in the fourth and fifth chapters—is that of God working through Christ (2 Cor 5:19) and placing him, as Christian theology has it, as the central figure in human history, even if the events described in the New Testament are not, in their totality, historically accurate.

> For God, who said, "Let light shine out of darkness," made his light shine in our hearts to give us the light of the knowledge of God's glory in the face of Christ. But we have this treasure in jars of clay to show that this all-surpassing power is from God and not us (2 Cor 4:6-7).

Wright does not deny this in his embrace of both history and faith, allowing each to have its say at their appropriate levels of discourse. In seeking credibility, a question of major proportion remains the extent to which the gap can extend between the historical Jesus and the Christ of faith, particularly if the former is to serve as a simultaneously opaque and perspicacious reflector through which the light of God, as revealed throughout the New Testament, illumines the latter. On this, Borg and Wright diverge, even as both acknowledge, in their different ways, the invariable tension and harmonization between the claims of history and those of faith. These issues go to the heart of *The Meaning of Jesus: Two Visions*.

2

Source Materials and the Christian Revelation

Borg

BORG REFERS TO THE gospels as "a developing tradition," "a mixture of history remembered and history metaphorised."[1] As he states it more fully:

> The gospels are the churches memories of the historical Jesus transformed by the community's experience and reflections in the decades after Easter. They therefore tell us what these early Christian communities had come to believe about Jesus by the last third of the first century. They are not, first and foremost, reports of the ministry itself.[2]

Wright does not object to Borg's depiction of the gospels as a developing tradition, even as for Borg, a much smaller core falls within the category of history as lived than it does for Wright. Particularly important for Borg is the sharp distinction between the Jesus of history that can be established by historical methodologies,

1. Borg and Wright, *Meaning of Jesus*, 4.
2. Borg, *Meeting Jesus Again for the First Time*, 10.

and that of the early Christian community, which placed pivotal texts into the mouth of the New Testament Jesus. For Borg, it is exceedingly unlikely that Jesus referred to himself as "the light of the world."[3] Rather, this was a metaphor used by the early church to signify that the risen Christ could be compared to light, even as this begs the broader issue as to what the vision of "light" actually referred. There are two issues in play.

The first is the imagery of the risen Christ in the gospel of John, in which the metaphor of light is but one symbol in a constellation of images. Thus, Christ was also the living water, the bread of life, and nothing less than God's own son through whom no person comes to the father except through him; elsewhere, the true vine. All of this imagery is grounded in the overarching belief announced in the prologue that in the beginning was the Word and that the Word became flesh and dwelt among us. However metaphorical John's language, there was something quite literal in the key claim that unless one is born again into the light of Christ "one cannot enter the kingdom of God" (John 3:5b). That claim is that in Christ the very "image of the invisible God" is manifest, in whom "all the fullness of the deity lives in bodily form" (Col 1:15, 2:9). A most related second issue is the question of who Jesus was and his self-defined purpose, for which Borg posits a significant difference between a pre- and post-Easter (which he conflates with a pre-and post-New Testament) vision; namely in the former, high Christological attributes do not pertain, even of Jesus as Israel's Messiah, which Borg, unlike Wright, rejects as an authentic self-perception of the historical personage.[4]

The "lenses" through which Borg constructs his interpretation of Jesus are those of critical historical scholarship and cultural

3. Borg and Wright, *Meaning of Jesus*, 5.

4. Since Borg views the constructed notion of the "historical Jesus" from a Jesus Seminar point of view, he interprets the composite NT picture of Jesus as reflecting a post-Easter phenomenon, while acknowledging pre-Easter—that is, authentically historical—threads that can be discerned, as more or less reliable. While acknowledging the imprint of the early church on the NT, Wright argues for a much greater continuity between the lived history of Jesus of Nazareth and the core narratives of the synoptic gospels, a case he argues for in much depth in *Christian Origins and the Question of God*, 2.

analysis, which he defines as "foundational."[5] Borg was raised in a traditional orthodox Protestant setting, which had a profound influence on his early Christian nurturance. His university training introduced him to the depth and richness of the secular intellectual world to which he gravitated for some considerable time.[6] In the process he became a scholar of the "historical Jesus" through which he grounded his intellectual identity, and to some degree, his personal being. This required rejection of what he viewed as the simplifications of his early faith stance, in which the Jesus of history and the Jesus portrayed in the New Testament, were viewed as synonymous figures. Borg ultimately came to discover the Christian revelation as an *experiential* reality in a manner that enabled him to transcend the dichotomy he felt between his earlier uncritical faith stance and his understanding of the scholarship on the historical Jesus, as reflected, largely, through the prism of the Jesus Seminar literature.[7]

The faith that Borg discovered anew "is the Jesus who is for us," which he is quick to point out, is not synonymous with any universal claim that Christ is the full embodiment of God in human flesh. Rather, "the gospels . . . are Christianity's primal narratives" because "these are the most important stories *we* (italics added) know, and we know them to be decisively true."[8] How Borg defines decisiveness is uncertain; based on what he has written, it can be reasonably surmised that he means something less than Christ is the full embodiment of God in human flesh as an ontological reality having universal significance. If he only means decisive for Christians, there is some question begging to consider; namely, in what sense and on what basis. Notwithstanding the insurmountable gap between the search and fulfillment, the issue of ultimate truth is a matter that requires substantial confrontation.

---

5. Borg and Wright, *Meaning of Jesus*, 8–9.

6. Ibid., 10.

7. See Borg, *Meeting Jesus Again for the First Time*, 3–15, for an autobiographical profile of his scholarly, theological, and spiritual odyssey. For a summary statement on the Jesus Seminar, see Funk, *Five Gospels*.

8. Borg, *Reading the Bible Again for the First Time*, 218.

Otherwise, the faith that he proclaims is, at bottom, an existential one that has no foundation beyond that collectively experienced by the Christian community over the centuries based on a mythological founding claim that points to something beyond itself toward an undefined universal significance working through, but transcendent of culture and language.

Viewed in this manner, Christianity has no more and no less truth claims than other religions, in which all the great faiths represent various communal pathways to the holy—an inexpressible holiness devoid, in the final analysis, of much specific content at the foundational level of meaning and significance. Thus, as Borg views it, Christianity shares an important affinity with Buddhism in respect to each of their "cultural-linguistic tradition[s] as both a response to the experience of the sacred and a mediator of such experiences."[9] The ultimate meaning of both of these religions transcends verbal description and dogma, in which words are but pointers to the ineffable. Consequently, Christianity, as one pathway to the holy, is, in principle, no more or no less valid than Buddhism, in which even the concept of God is but a pointer to that which can only transcend verbal description.[10]

On Borg's account, the risen Christ is ultimately a symbol—a most profound one—for the breaking in of God in human experience, in which other religious traditions and other symbols will equally do in their opening different dimensions of the holy to their various practitioners. The radical particularity of Christianity is, therefore relativized in the pluralism of a global reality, in which there are various pathways to the truth, a concept that remains highly underdeveloped in Borg's theology.

---

9. Borg, *Jesus and Buddha*, xvi.

10. In a broader statement, Borg argues that Jesus "is one of many mediators of the sacred." Noting that such a perception "subtracts from the uniqueness of Jesus and the Christian tradition, it also . . . adds to the credibility of both." In this, Borg rejects the "popular Christian usage [on] the 'uniqueness' of Jesus [that] is most commonly tied to the notion that he is uniquely an exclusively true revelation of God." Borg and Wight, *Meeting Jesus Again for the First Time*, 37, 45, n. 42.

Wright

As he notes, Wright is subject to criticism from both secular historians and from certain schools of evangelical and Reformed theology. Secular academics have grounds to question Wright for allowing the presuppositions of faith to influence his interpretation of early Christianity. Biblical theologians may have concerns about the wisdom of Wright's extensive reliance on the discipline of history in firming up a stance that is ultimately based on faith. Wright acknowledges that the epistemological bases of faith and historical studies are grounded in fundamentally different presuppositions. With this proviso, he draws extensively on history as a profoundly important penultimate resource in linking faith to solid human experience.

One of Wright's more proximate concerns is the dualism in contemporary intellectual history, in which religious faith, as an epistemological category, has no grounds of legitimacy in the secular academy. The ghettoization operates in both ways to the extent that theologians cloister themselves by placing a ring around faith that is not subject to rational argument, as defined by the rigorous—though ultimately limited—categories of secular scholarship. Wright seeks to reconcile the two in order to escape the "attic (faith divorced from history) and the dungeon (history divorced from faith)"[11]. Through his massive research project, Wright has found a great deal of symmetry between historical reconstruction and the claims of the gospels and the letters of Paul, which he elaborates upon to some degree in *The Meanings of Jesus*.

This is a primary difference with Borg, who, in contrast to Wright, points to the radical divergences between academic research on the historical Jesus and his existentialist rediscovery of Jesus anew. Because he lacks an epistemological basis for a more direct embrace of the historical validity of the biblical narrative, for Borg, faith claims can be only interpreted through metaphorical and mythological prisms. Based on Borg's epistemology, any reconciliation with the thought world of modern scholarship

11. Ibid., 16.

needs to take into account his grounding point, in which religious beliefs, based on doctrinal or given biblical statements, are not in themselves, subject to critical scholarly investigation.[12]

Viewing faith without history and history without faith as barren, Wright argues that the relationship between the two is ultimately dialectical, "a no-holds barred history, on the one hand and a no-holds barred faith, on the other."[13] Their mutual power is that each speaks from the vantage point of its own unique idiom, whether in convergence or in opposition to one another. Even over interpretative problems of a highly obdurate nature, Wright has sometimes "found that by living with the problem, turning it this way and that in the complex and hidden world of personal and communal consciousness and reflection, faith has been able to discover not just that the new, and initially surprising historical evidence, was capable of being accommodated." Even more, "by looking at the challenge from all angles," he sometimes found that "historical evidence was as well if not better interpreted within a different framework"[14] opened up through the standpoint of faith than that provided by the academic guild of history and critical biblical scholarship. Thus for Wright, the study of history has confirmed some of the deepest claims of faith, even while acknowledging that, in the final analysis, faith cannot be substantiated by historical consciousness and secondary evidence. Wright notes, but underplays this reality.

12. In reflecting on the chasm between his earlier, pre-critical belief in the basic gospel story and his post-critical understanding of faith, based on the historically deconstructive work of the Jesus Seminar, Borg calls for a return to the original Greek and Latin understanding of beliefs as something other than "a set of doctrines or teachings." Rather than relying on doctrine as a first order definition of what a belief consists of, "believing in Jesus . . . . means [first and foremost] to give one's heart, one's self at its deepest level, to the post-Easter Jesus who is the living Lord, the side of God turned toward us, the face of God, the Lord who is also the Spirit." Borg and Wright, *Meeting Jesus Again for the First Time*, 137. According to Borg, it is not information we need about Jesus, but a living relationship, a dichotomy that is rejected by Wright and a vast array of evangelical theologians and biblical scholars.

13. Borg and Wright, *Meaning of Jesus*, 18.

14. Ibid., 17,

In approaching Wright's historical methodology let us note what he critiques, as well as that for which he advocates. Namely, his target is nothing less than the mainstream orthodoxies of historical biblical criticism, particularly the "belief that isolated fragments of Jesus material circulated, and developed, in the early church divorced from narrative frameworks,"[15] as reflected, for example, in source and redaction criticism. The problem with much of this scholarship is its limited evidentiary basis, in which its underlying methodology presupposes key assumptions, particularly a wide gulf between the historical Jesus and his first followers, and the traditions of the early church, as embodied in the gospel texts.

Wright argues that there is not sufficient evidence to definitively know all the key factors to distinguish accurately between original events and later retrojections. Thus, without knowing the narrative framework in which the fragmentary texts were initially embedded, making definitive statements about whether they were early or late is, at best, problematic. He proposes another approach; namely, starting with what we do know and building systematically toward reasoned, evidentiary-based conclusions in filling in the gaps as much as possible, a methodology he describes as "inference to the best explanation" (italics removed).[16] A key starting point for Wright is the currently available knowledge of Jesus, derived mostly from the New Testament, that he "was a Jewish prophet announcing the kingdom of God." On that, we are on more solid ground than "what we know about the history of traditions that led up to the gospels as we have them."[17] Based on this grounding framework, the method that Wright proposes is "to draw in more and more of the evidence within a growing hypothesis about Jesus himself and Christian writings, *including the writing of the gospels*" (cited italics highlighted in original unless otherwise noted).[18]

---

15. Ibid., 23.

16. Wright, *Christian Origins and the Question of God*, 3:716.

17. Borg and Wright, *Meaning of Jesus*, 23.

18. Ibid.

Wright's hypothesis is that Jesus of Nazareth understood himself to be Israel's Messiah, his earliest followers perceived him as such, and both acted accordingly. Closely related is Wright's assumption that the resurrection motif was accepted very early on, as reflected in the writings of Paul. This is part of his contention that the evidence is stronger that the depiction of the empty tomb and the resurrection sightings, as described in the gospels, reflected more of what actually happened than arguments to the contrary that seek to dismiss these phenomena as a post-Easer fabrication of the early church.[19] Building on these assumptions in his various books, Wright has sought to work through the following expanding set of questions through "the scientific method of hypothesis and verification:"[20]

> What can be known about Jesus? Where does he belong in the world of his day (the world of Greek-Roman antiquity and of first-century Judaism in particular)? What were his aims, and to what extent did he accomplish them? What caused him to meet an early death? Why did a movement claiming allegiance to him spring up shortly after his death, taking a shape that was both like and significantly unlike other movements of the time?[21]

As a "big picture" Christian historian, Wright maintains that focusing on these more fundamental questions will cumulatively provide a clearer picture of the historical Jesus than currently available through much of the fragmented textual criticism that undergirds Protestant liberal critical scholarship. It is this critically realist scientific approach that Wright posits against the Jesus

---

19. See Wright, *Christian Origins and the Question of God*, 3:3–31, 685–713, for a substantial overview of Wright's argument on the historical viability of the resurrection sightings. The first chapter includes a summary statement "that the *only* possible reason why early Christianity began and took shape as it did is that the tomb really was empty and that people really did meet Jesus alive again, and . . . that though admitting it involves accepting a challenge at the level of world view itself, the best historical explanation . . . is that Jesus was indeed bodily raised from the dead." Ibid., 8.

20. Borg and Wright, *Meaning of Jesus*, 22.

21. Ibid., 19.

Seminar, in which Borg, along with Crossan, are leading lights, in the radical gulf its proponents depict between the historical Jesus and the constructed NT Christ of the early church.[22] Of course, Wright has his own presuppositions, while Borg and Crossan have marshaled more than a little evidence on behalf of their scholarship. Consequently, Wright might be a little less than fair in his broad brushed critique of the critical biblical scholarship extending back to the late nineteenth century. Nonetheless, on the historical Jesus and the rise of the early church, his cumulative research is substantial. Moreover, he offers the tantalizing prospect that there may be considerably more congruence between the historical figure of Jesus of Nazareth and the Christ of faith than that accepted in most of the critical scholarship, even as he is not always appreciative as he might be of the potentially persistent gulf between the two.

It may be both a source of enlightenment and a profound source of temptation in giving as much weight as Wright does to history. Wright is on solid ground in pointing to the need to work

22. Wright positions critical realism as an epistemological midpoint between the ineradicable subjectivity of phenomenology and the alleged objectivism of positivism. He maintains that such a reading "will recognize, and take fully into account, the perspective of the reader." It will also "insist that, within the story or stories that seem to make sense of the whole of reality . . . texts . . . can be read . . . that have a life and set of appropriate meanings . . . independent of their . . . their reader." Such texts even extend beyond authorial intent in addressing "the deepest level of meaning . . . [inherent] in the [the biblical] stories, and ultimately the worldviews, which the texts thus articulate." Wright, *Christian Origins and the Question of God*, 1:66. More as a whisper than a stated fact, Wright's implication is that God is the ultimate author of the biblical narrative who works within and through the texts, within and through the various historical contexts in which they took shape and in which they continue to speak, based on their ultimately revelatory standing. The proof of any such supposition is beyond what can be discerned through exacting historical analysis. Nonetheless, the biblical narrative contains a transcendent reference that works within and beyond specific writers and readers of the text that Wright seeks to tease out with as much discernment as possible through a critical realist methodology based on best-case hypothesis formation, supportive evidence, and critical evaluation of alternative explanations. For a more technical study of critical realist philosophy and methodology, see, Archer, et al., *Critical Realism*.

against any polarity between the attic of faith without history and the dungeon of history without faith. Nonetheless, there may be less need for integration than simply further light in our looking through a mirror, dimly in the ongoing pilgrimage, in which our meat is nothing more and nothing less than the daily manna of enhanced knowledge provided to us through both formal research and the medium of faith.

3

The Historical Jesus and Israel's Messiah

Borg

IN VIEWING THE NEW Testament as a combination of "history remembered" and history "metaphorized," Borg posits a radical disjuncture between the Jesus of history and the Christ of faith. Specifically, the notion of Jesus as Israel's Messiah was a product of the early church rather than a contemporary reflection of Jesus' self-perception. Since Jesus did not embrace this category for himself, neither, posits Borg, did he view a martyred death as central to his vocation.[1] Accordingly, the "exalted titles" accompanying the church's depiction of Jesus as Messiah, are "exalted metaphors."[2] Behind and beneath these metaphors was the living presence of Jesus as a spirit filled person mediating the presence of God, pointing beyond language, toward "deeper" truths that first century Judaism could, at best, only partially embody.

---

1. Borg and Wright, *Meaning of Jesus*, 54.
2. Ibid., 53.

In Borg's view, Jesus, as a historical personage, was primarily a teacher, healer, social prophet, and "spirit person,"[3] in many respects, the "liberal" Jesus of the late nineteenth century. The categories Borg draws upon to characterize the historical Jesus are based less on Jewish history and Scripture, per se, "than cross-cultural study of types of religious personality"[4] that may be as applicable to Buddhism as to Judaism or to early Christianity. The broader point that Borg makes is that while the categories that he draws on "are not specifically Jewish," and neither is "the language . . . specifically biblical," they nonetheless have roots in deep Jewish tradition.[5] On this interpretation, both Judaism and Christianity may be viewed as "axial" religions, in which their commonalities in an overarching quest for the universal god are considered more fundamentally important than surface and not so surface differences.[6] For Borg, this includes rejection of "supernatural theism" as a viable concept "for thinking about God's relationship to the world,"[7] as well as any scandal of particularity that God is most fully revealed in a given religious "myth" or "metaphor."

As Borg views it, Jesus' primary vocation was that of "Jewish mystic."[8] This is fundamentally what Borg means when he describes Jesus as a "spirit person," terms he used interchangeably. Borg draws much on contemporary spirituality in this depiction. Thus, with other mystics, Jesus "had decisive and . . . firsthand experiences of the sacred."[9] Such "'eyes closed' mystical states" include "ineffability," which cannot be explained "in ordinary language but only with the language of metaphor." There is also a transient nature to such experiences and also much "passivity" in that "they are received rather than achieved." In addition, there is, in Jesus, a sense of the "noetic" based on what is sometimes

3. Ibid.
4. Ibid., 60
5. Ibid.
6. Armstrong, "Religion: What's God got to do with it?"
7. Borg and Wright, *Meaning of Jesus*, 62.
8. Ibid., 64.
9. Ibid., 60.

referred to as conative or embodied knowledge that accompanies these experiences. These are not just "strong feelings" which are crucial to mystical experience, but *knowledge* of the spiritual realm that in some determinative way, requires undergoing to fully obtain. Borg's final depiction is the category of the "transformative," in which the mystic is fundamentally changed as a result of such undergoing.[10] It is this spirit person that most closely conforms to the Jesus as lived, as disclosed in the sources and in the prevailing interpretations of modern biblical scholarship when the New Testament overlay of Jesus as the Jewish Messiah is peeled back. This Jesus was still Jewish in every way, which provided the religious tradition that shaped the categories of his mystical experience.

Based on this interpretation, in which the Jesus of history and the Christ of the New Testament diverge in radical respects, the Jesus that Borg discerns was principally a "healer, wisdom teacher, social prophet, and movement initiator."[11] The scandalous question Borg indirectly puts to more orthodox interpretations is, "had Jesus lived and taught for forty more years as the Buddha did, what more might we be able to discern about his purpose?"[12] Thus, not only was the cross a tragically inessential aspect of the life and meaning of Jesus of Nazareth for Jewish, and ultimately, world history. Borg's implicit message is that neither is it the crucial event in our own interpretation and appropriation of the wisdom and teaching of Jesus in our lives.

Borg views the healing narratives in the gospels as having "programmatic significance," as signs of Jesus pointing to the breaking in of the kingdom of God. In illustrating their metaphorical significance Borg, drawing on the Q tradition, references Matthew 11:4, in which Jesus is reported to have said:

> Go and tell John what you hear and see: the blind receive
> their sight and the lame walk, lepers are cleansed and the

---

10. Ibid., 61.

11. Ibid., 65.

12. Ibid. 67.

deaf here [sic], and the dead are raised up, and the poor
have good news preached to them[13]

Borg notes that such healing "points to a time of deliverance,"[14]
but bypasses the context in which Jesus addresses John; namely,
John's question, "Are you the one who to come or should we expect
someone else?" (Matt 11:3). On this reading, healings do have metaphorical significance in symbolizing the breaking in of the kingdom
of God; however, according to the gospel writers, in a manner in
which, to use a well-known aphorism, "the proclaimer is also the
proclaimed" as Israel's Messiah. To be fair, Borg's main objective in
this particular section is to illustrate the importance of healing in
Jesus' ministry, as part of his broader objective throughout chapter
four, to describe the pre-Easter (that is, pre-New Testament) Jesus,
as best that can be discerned by the evidence, shaped by the interpretive grids through which his analysis is sifted. On this reading,
particularly through dominant modes of source, form, and redaction criticism, Borg can only draw the conclusion that Jesus, as Israel's Messiah, was a New Testament retrojection.

Unquestionable proof about Jesus' consciousness is, as
Borg and Wright note, beyond determination through available
evidence. Whether the intellectual mindset through which Borg
discovers Jesus anew allows him to rigorously examine Wright's
hypothesis that the messianic identity of Jesus of Nazareth is not
only historically plausible, but the most likely explanation of the
available evidence, is another matter. This is an issue of considerable importance, since any such self-consciousness, as Wright
argues, would have played a major role not only in the textual construction of the New Testament Jesus, but in very the formation of
the historical personage, in the shaping of the mission of the one
who lived and died in a specific time and place.[15]

13. Ibid., 67. Borg acknowledges uncertainty as to "whether this saying
goes back to Jesus." His broader point is that the passage "indicates how the
mighty deeds of Jesus were seen by the time of Q: as signs that the time of
deliverance spoken of by Isaiah had arrived," (ibid., 260, n. 37).

14. Ibid., 67.

15. Clearly, Borg is skeptical. As he states, in critiquing "the popular image

So what was Jesus up to? This is the question that Borg seeks to answer in chapter four. As someone who shattered "conventional wisdom," Jesus provided "a new way of seeing," "a new way of centering" (italics removed),[16] in which "he taught a path of transformation centered in the sacred." It was within this context of teacher that Jesus defined his core mission as "social prophet" and "movement initiator." As a social prophet, Jesus cast his lot with the poor, the outcast, the "marginalized." In this prophetic mission, Jesus sought to counteract the "politics of oppression" (that of Rome's and the Jewish religious aristocracy), the "economics of exploitation" (against the power of the "urban ruling elites"), and the "religion of legitmation" of the ruling Jewish class.[17] In building on the legacy of John the Baptist, Borg views Jesus' most fundamental mission as that of proclaiming the kingdom of God through the vision of the inverted world, in which the last ones now shall later be first.

For Borg, the vision of Jesus as a "prophet of the kingdom of God," symbolized by the promise of the redemption of Israel to its rightful relationship with its maker, is a potent metaphor. It is "as equally good as . . . [his] own crystallization, 'Jesus as Jewish mystic.'"[18] The latter is more accurate in keeping in mind the transcultural, metaphorical nature of such imagery, where for Borg, higher levels of ultimate reality reside. Otherwise, argues Borg, the scandal of particularity, even of Jewish monotheism, as depicted throughout the Bible, becomes conflated for a more universal understanding of reality, which, if literally accepted, denies such equal legitimacy for other religious perspectives. Borg can say the following about Jesus of Nazareth:

. . . the self-understanding and message of the pre-Easter Jesus were in all likelihood *nonmessianic*." He bases this on the assumption that the Jesus of history "pointed away from himself to God," in which the proclaimer was emphatically not the proclaimed. Borg, *Meeting Jesus Again for the First Time*, 29.

16. Borg and Wright, *Meaning of Jesus*, 70.

17. Ibid., 71–72.

18. Ibid., 75.

He knew how to heal. He knew how to create memorable sayings and stories; he had a metaphoric mind. He knew that God was accessible to the marginalized because he was from the marginalized himself. He knew that tradition and convention were not sacred in themselves but, at best, pointers to and mediators of the sacred and, at worst, a snare. He knew an oppressive and exploitative social order that legitimated itself in the name of God, and he knew this was not God's will. And he knew all of this most foundationally because he knew God[19]

What Borg cannot say is that Jesus of Nazareth was, or viewed himself as, Israel's Messiah, not only proclaiming the kingdom of God, but the primary agent through whom the realm of God would be ushered in both within Israel and throughout the world. What Borg most emphatically cannot say is that Jesus is God incarnate in human flesh, except in the most metaphorical sense, given the unfathomable gap between language and concrete historico-cultural experience underlying first-century Israel. Rather, Jesus was a pointer, an exceedingly profound symbol of the righteousness of God, which is manifest in different forms and personages in other cultures and times. It was this Jesus that Borg rediscovered, who, *for him* and for countless others—particularly Christian seekers that are reluctant to embrace the major tenets of the orthodox theological tradition—mediates universal truth and God's most profound love. Borg does not want to deny the same level of depth to other religious traditions, which have their own symbols and metaphors for conveying in language that can only falter the universal search for truth and holiness, which, in its profoundest depictions, remains inscrutable.

Wright

Wright does not categorically dismiss the depiction of Jesus' mission identified by Borg, although he does not find it especially useful. Rather, he roots Jesus' mission firmly in the thought world

19. Ibid., 76.

of Second Temple Judaism to explain what Jesus sought to accomplish. At its foundation was his "belief that Israel had been chosen to be YHWH's special people through whom the world would be addressed by its creator."[20] That is, on Jesus' interpretation, the universality of God's truth is revealed fully, and nowhere else than in the Lord, our God, depicted throughout the Jewish scriptures. That truth, as Jesus would have understood it, is neither a too distant "up in heaven reality" nor an impenetrable phenomenon "beyond the sea." Neither is it "too mysterious" for human understanding. Rather, the truth to which Jesus referred, the singular truth, "is very near you, it is in your mouth and in your heart that you may obey it" (Deut 30:11–14). This singular truth was revealed by Israel's God in the "commandments and . . . decrees that are written in this Book of the law" (Deut 30:10a).

It was this law that Jesus radically brought to prophetic culmination rather than abolishing it (Matt 5:17) through his healing, teaching, movement building, and ultimately through the agency of his own calling as Israel's Messiah. This is Wright's key thesis. Whatever validity in Borg's depiction, any effort to reconstruct the historical Jesus through modern categories like spirit person, social prophet, or movement initiator, without a clear focus on the eschatology that undergirded his mission is to be tinged with a degree of presentism that occludes as much, if not more, than what it discloses about the historical personage. So argues Wright.

In concurrence with Borg's broader understanding, Israel acknowledged "the secret things belong[ing] to the Lord our God" (Deut 29:29a) well beyond human language and comprehension. The more substantial issue remains that the heart of Israel's religion was not based on a universality that could be readily transferred to the metaphors and symbols of other cultures and times. "First-century Jewish monotheis[ts]" across the theological landscape viewed such cross-cultural sensibility of seeking commonalities rather than positing sharp differences between Israel's God and

---

20. Ibid., 32.

other revelations as idolatry—"either concrete creations of human hands or abstract creations of human minds."[21]

Notwithstanding the ineffable mystery beyond human understanding, as referenced in both testaments, the heart of Israel's religion centered on "those things which are revealed [that] belong to us and to our children forever" (Deut: 29:29b)—the heart and center of Scripture—the grounding source of Judaism and Christianity. The Word is no mere metaphor or symbol pointing beyond its actual referent, wherein for Borg resides its ultimate significance. Rather, it is the means itself, through which the revelation of God takes place. While there are those "secret things" about God's truth beyond human comprehension, the focal point of Israel's religion and the mission of Jesus centered on the "things [that are] revealed" (Deut 29:29b) and the necessity of pursing such truth with the entirety of one's "heart and . . . soul" (Deut 30:10b). Without that unified level of commitment, at least in intention, the specter of worshipping the creation rather than the creator, which invariably haunts the human heart, becomes the basis for unbelief rather than any lack of knowledge itself. According to Scripture, the latter is a by-product of idolatry, in an all-too-human desire to escape from the responsibilities and consequences of adherence to the covenant with the living God (Rom 1:21–23).

According to Wright, belief in the radical particularity and superiority of the living God, revealed in and through Israel's Scripture, grounded everything that was essential about Jesus' mission. While granting some validity to Borg's modernist categories, Wright argues that reference to Jesus as a "spirit person" or even "Jewish mystic" lacks the specificity of who Jesus was in the highly particular context of his times. More pointedly, intimates Wright, any interpretation of the historical Jesus not deeply seeped in the language and beliefs surrounding Second Temple Judaism are profoundly flawed. So, what was this "Palestinian Jew"[22] up to according to Wright? In broad strokes, Wright follows along the trajectory of Borg's five point depiction, but fills in the descrip-

---

21. Ibid., 31.
22. Ibid., 35.

tion with the specificity of Jesus' distinctive first-century, Second Temple, eschatological, Jewish identity.

First and foremost, Jesus was a "first century Jewish prophet" (italics removed), a "second temple"[23] religious leader whose mission embodied the imagery of exile and return, as exhibited in the political and religious imagination of the period among a wide array of groups. Among those seeking a restoration of Israel's greatness in a return to God's calling of a holy people, the imagery of "new exodus"[24] took on a significant role. In typological analogy to the Babylonian captivity, with its corresponding quest for a geographical return to a redeemed Israel, the restoration in the later Second Temple period combined an internal cleansing with a call for the decisive eradication of the domination of Rome, in a perspective in which politics and theology were complexly intertwined.

It was within this context that "Jesus spoke of himself as a prophet . . . behaved as a prophet, and when others referred to him in this way he did not correct them."[25] More than a "spirit person," or even "Jewish mystic," Jesus was a prophet in the mode of Isaiah, with sharply articulated Jewish connotations based on the imagery of exile, an internal one, in the Second Temple period—"a first-century Jewish prophet *announcing God's kingdom*."[26] Restoration to something pointed to in times of old, but never achieved was at the heart of the Second Temple vision—God's full indwelling within the nation of Israel, in which the redeemed nation becomes the servant for expanding God's kingdom throughout the world. As Wright describes it, the kingdom Jesus proclaimed "denoted not a *place* where God ruled, but rather the fact that God ruled—or, rather, the *fact* that he would soon rule, because he was certainly not doing so" during the time of his earthly ministry "in the way he intended to do so."[27]

23. Ibid., 33.
24. Ibid., 32.
25. Ibid., 33.
26. Ibid.
27. Ibid.

Jesus' understanding of God embodied the ineffable, transient, noetic, and transformative dimensions of spiritual reality, as described by Borg. Yet, for Jesus, such experiences were disclosures of the presence of God revealed in Israel's most evocative literature, which resided, and resided only, for Jesus, in Israel's founding revelation. It was this religion Jesus sought to revitalize, and, on Wright's interpretation, to bring to dynamic fulfillment through the agency of his own personage.

One could draw on the categories Borg uses in his depiction of Jesus to get a handle on what he was up to. Yet, if taken as the summation of religious experience they reflect a sort of empty universality in which the specific context of any particular religion are evaluated not on their own terms, but on how they measure up to the more intangible depictions of Borg's preferred categories. Truth claims based on a set of biblical and theological beliefs, or doctrines, are, according to Borg, subordinate to what Tillich identifies as the "ultimate concern" underlying the ineffable phenomenon of experience, which is beyond the capacity of language to describe, although it can be pointed to metaphorically. According to Wright, the proclamation of the kingdom of God in the restoration of Israel's most fundamental calling as a light onto the Gentiles, is what drove this "Galilean Jewish peasant"[28] to the ultimate commitment that led to the cross.

Without this radical specificity at the heart of Second Temple Judaism and emergent Christianity, faith becomes subordinate to a constellation of experiential categories that then professes to be the basis for religious universality. The religion of Israel, grounded so extensively in the written word and the dynamic, historically influenced inter-textual shaping of an emerging, and ultimately, enduring New Testament canon, becomes, on Borg's interpretation, a metaphor—of a profound sort, to be sure—for a more universal truth, in principle, transculturally accessible through other images, stories, and doctrines based on other religious traditions. By contrast, as Wright understands it, the symbols, language, and historical unfolding of Israel's biblical story, carried for Jesus of Nazareth full

28. Ibid., 59.

significance on its own terms through which he encountered the ineffable, whom he named, and for whom he lived and died, namely, Abba Father, the Lord our God, the holy one of Israel.

The third and most fundamental of Wright's claims about the historical Jesus was "that the kingdom [of God] was breaking into Israel's history in and through his own presence" (italics removed),[29] as the long awaited Messiah. In line with a broad stream of critical biblical scholarship, it is this claim, in particular, that Borg rejects, which in turn grounds his proclivity to posit a great divide between the Jesus of history and the Christ of faith. Wright notes that the issue over the consciousness of Jesus lacks sufficient empirical verification to claim as an established fact. Nonetheless, he puts forward a hypothesis on what he discerns as the most likely conclusion, based on the available evidence, particularly when one is not locked into the paradigmatic assumptions of the broad stream of contemporary liberal biblical scholarship, rooted in historical and hermeneutical issues extending back to the eighteenth and nineteenth centuries.[30] This included not simply the brute claim of the kingdom of God, but the nature of the kingdom proclaimed, based on a suffering Messiah who conquered, but only by way of the cross.

The cross was the pathway not only of the Messiah, but representative of the paradigmatic suffering a redemptive Israel needed to undergo, as initially reflected in the temptations Jesus faced in the desert. Namely, Jesus' repudiation of Satan's temptations was a call for radical obedience to God to the point of surrendering all semblance of national glorification; embracing instead, the truer vocation of the Suffering Servant, in which God, and God only, would bring to magnificent consummation his kingdom, in his time when the fullness of the Gentiles were brought in. On Jesus' messianic vision, Israel was called, but enjoyed no special privileges other than the mandate to be faithful to the call to the point of death of any vestige of national triumphalism. That death to glorification is what Jesus mirrored in and through his own

29. Ibid., 37.
30. Frei, *Eclipse of Biblical Narrative*.

ministry, in which Israel—the redeemed Israel of the New Covenant—symbolically became the Suffering Servant in carrying out what the nation had not been able to achieve through obedience to the law. It was in this sense that the blood of the Lamb took on and took away the sins of the world, in which the Messiah became the preeminent mediator to the pathway that would lead to full consummation in Israel redeemed.[31] The kingdom of God would reign on earth in the era of New Israel symbolized in the temple cleansing actions of Jesus of Nazareth, who, as Messiah, "would replace the temple"[32] as the new focal point of true worship.[33]

31. Wright argues that the initial focus of the atonement "was not, first and foremost, a way of saying that the moral failures of individuals had been atoned for in some abstract theological transaction." He notes that an individual atonement theology would soon emerge "in Paul's mature thought," though not one that negated the realm of the social and political, which extended to creation, itself (Rom 8:19–25). The original "claim [was] about what Israel's God had done, in fulfillment of the scriptural prophecies, to bring Israel's long night of exile to its conclusion, to deal with Israel's 'sins' that had kept Israel enslaved to the pagan powers of the world, and to bring about the real 'return from exile,' the dawn of the new day, for which Israel had longed." The earliest Christians viewed the death and resurrection of Jesus "as the hinge upon which the door of God's new world had swung open." Through the sacrifice of Christ, "the sins that caused Israel's exile had now been dealt with, and the time of forgiveness had arrived." Borg and Wright, *Meaning of Jesus*, 103. With the mission to the Gentiles, the work of the atonement expanded in the sense that "what God did for Israel he does in some sense for the whole world." Ibid., 104. In this, the victory of God in Christ was not just about defeating the power of Rome, but the power of evil, itself, through the countervailing power of the Suffering Servant masked as weakness (1 Cor 1:20–28). More expansive theories of the atonement would follow that would transform Christianity into a universal religion. What Wright does not want us to lose sight of is that later developments built on the original focus of the restoration of Israel in new exodus rather than issuing in something radically new—an invention of the late first-century church.

32. Borg and Wright, *Meaning of Jesus*, 45.

33. As Wright further explains, "Jesus' temple action was an acted parable of judgment." In this, Wright argues that Jesus, in enacting the role of the great prophets, presaged the destruction of the temple by Rome. Such judgment "would be followed by the establishment of the messianic community, focused on Jesus himself, that would replace the temple once and for all." *Meaning of Jesus*, 45. Noting the symbolic "claim, that in his work *the temple* was being rebuilt," Wright maintains that the "metaphor denoted something concrete,

What Wright argues is that, given the temper of the times and all that contemporary scholarship discloses of the period, there was nothing in the nature of those times that would have impeded Jesus' self-identification as Israel's Messiah, "charged by Israel's God with inaugurating the kingdom."[34] Rather, there was much to support it based on the trajectory of his mission and the logical conclusions that could be drawn out from it. The NT depiction has, on Wright's view, a much more substantial historical core than that posited by Borg and his Jesus Seminar associates. In Borg's depiction of the NT Jesus, there is a nucleus in history—history remembered; more fundamentally, history metaphorized. With Wright there is much greater symmetry between history as lived and faith as received, notwithstanding the inevitable, though far from unfathomable chasm, between the two.[35]

---

namely Jesus himself and his community and movement" (ibid., 46), in which his entire ministry was suffused with such symbolic action pointing to "new exodus." For a perspective critical of the emphasis Wright places on the temple cleansing, see Stein, "N. T. Wright's *Jesus and the Victory of God.*"

34. Borg and Wright, *Meaning of Jesus*, 39.

35. See Wright, *Christian Origins and the Question of God*, 2:477–538 for Wright's most extensive statement on the messianic consciousness of Jesus of Nazareth.

4

Christology

Borg

BORG AND WRIGHT ACCEPT the basic Christian proclamation that "Jesus lives" as "both Lord and Christ.[1]" For Borg, these affirmations reflect the simple fact that "the followers of Jesus, then and now, continued to experience Jesus as a living reality after his death."[2] Whatever actually happened during the ministry of Jesus and in the events surrounding the reports of the empty tomb and the post-crucifixion sightings of the risen Messiah, it is the risen Christ "encountered as a living spiritual reality" which is the grounding point of faith for Borg, upon which the authenticity of doctrine and tradition are legitimized as metaphorical expressions for truths that ultimately transcend the boundaries of language.

Wright accepts Borg's thesis that the full incarnational view of Jesus as the son of God was a product of "a developing tradition,"[3] while identifying three interrelated strands that were extant very early on in both pre- and post-Easter manifestations, though

1. Borg and Wright, *Meaning of Jesus*, 129.
2. Ibid., 135.
3. Ibid., 130.

obviously more fully developed in the latter. The first, in line with the early church, is that Jesus perceived himself as Israel's Messiah. The second was that Jesus identified the Messiah as "Israel's true king," "the true monarch of the gentile world." Wright identifies the third early representation of Jesus, as "the personal embodiment and revelation *of* the one true god."[4] In Wright's elaboration of the last point:

> Jesus of Nazareth was conscious of a vocation: a vocation given him by the one he knew as 'father', to enact in himself what, in Israel's scriptures, God had promised to accomplish all by himself. He would be the pillar of cloud and fire for the people of the new exodus. He would embody in himself the returning and redeeming action of the covenant God.[5]

Because he is suspicious of any such claims, Borg does not envision a strong fit between Jesus as the Jewish Messiah, as identified by himself and his initial followers—both before and after the crucifixion—as does Wright, and the fully formed Christ of the New Testament, the suffering and risen Lord of human history (Phil 2:9–11). In Borg's view, the death and resurrection of the Christ of faith point to a metaphorical meaning; that of "dying to an old way of being and being born into a new way of being"—a way that "is known in all of the religions of the world."[6] Based on the dichotomy he draws between thought and experience, Borg contends that "the way of Jesus is not [based on] a set of beliefs about Jesus." Rather, it is based on a *relationship* with the living God through identification with Christ in a manner that "stimulates a transition and transformation from an old way of being to a new way of being,"[7] a pathway that is available through a broad array of religious and secular traditions.

---

4. Wright, *Christian Origins and the Question of God*, 3:723–37. Citations are taken from 729 and 731. See Wright, *Christian Origins and the Question of God*, 2:477–662, for Jesus' self-identification as Messiah and Son of God.

5. Wright, *Christian Origins and the Question of God*, 2:653.

6. Borg, *Reading the Bible Again for the First Time*, 216.

7. Ibid., 216–17.

Consequently, for Borg, the various referencing of Jesus in the New Testament, whether as "The Wisdom of God" "The Son of God," or "messiah," point metaphorically to the same existential reality; that of "tak[ing] very seriously what we see in him as a disclosure of God."[8] By contrast, Wright argues that an implicit incarnational perspective was assumed as early as Paul (particularly, 1 Cor 8:6 and Phil 2:5–11), based on the grounding belief that God's will, in full bodily form, was exhibited in the life, teaching, and the symbolism of the healings, along with the crucifixion and resurrection of Jesus of Nazareth. As Paul might have expressed it, through the echoed voice of Wright:

> If you start with the God of the Exodus, of Isaiah, of creation and covenant, and of the psalms, and ask what God might look like were he to become human, you will find that he might look very much like Jesus of Nazareth, and perhaps never more so than when he dies on a Roman cross.[9]

This Jesus, perceived as Israel's Messiah, interpreted through the prism of Isaiah's Suffering Servant, implicit in the cited Pauline texts, and amplified more fully in the Gospel of John, Acts, Colossians, and Hebrews, laid the basis for a more fully developed incarnational perspective of the later first-century church, in which the core elements were very early grounded.

My critique of Borg's position is not that the New Testament does not use metaphor, but the significance between the images evoked and that to which the images refer, namely to Jesus the Christ as "the image of the invisible God" upon whom "all the fullness of the Deity lives in bodily form" (Col 1:15, 2:9). With Borg, the metaphorical reality beneath this language has universal significance beyond the thought categories of Second Temple Judaism, and even fully formed Christological ones, in their symbolic pointing toward a more transcendent and universal reality than that which can be depicted in words. For Wright, they emerge from

8. Ibid., 152.
9. Ibid., 167.

their grounding in Jesus' messianic vocation, in which fully formed Christological claims only make sense to the extent to which they maintain their rooting in the creation narrative, the Abrahamic covenant, the wisdom literature, and the apocalyptic longing for full restoration with God, rooted in Israel's exodus story. The force of Wright's argument cannot be used to substantiate what actually happened in the first few years after Jesus' death. However, it does lend support to counteracting the notion that the view of Jesus, as both Israel's Messiah and the Lord of human history (Phil 2:9–11), was a product of a later faith community, which the gospel writers retrojected into history through their narrative constructions.

Borg and Wright agree that the Christian revelation was not simply a product of the imagination of Jesus, or of the events and beliefs surrounding his life, teaching, death, and resurrection, nor even simply a product of the early faith community and the writings of the texts that ultimately took canonical shape in the New Testament. For both writers, all of these events are crucial for understanding the emergence of first century Christianity. What both writers would also say is that it was (and is) God working through these events which brought to proximate fulfillment in the mission to the Gentiles, God's covenant with Abraham, as depicted in Genesis 12. Where Borg and Wright differ is in the extent to which they perceive the events depicted in the New Testament, as historically accurate and the extent to which the claims of faith are continuous or discontinuous with that history.

For Borg, the importance of the resurrection is "that the risen Christ journeys with us"[10] throughout our lives. The cost, as well as the joy, is in following Jesus "on the path of death and resurrection,"[11] regardless as to the literal truth of the biblical narrative. It is this death and rebirth imagery that Calvary, in its most fundamental sense, signifies. It is in this profound mirroring of the pathway to new life in unswerving faith in God that Jesus, as Christ, "becomes the incarnation of the Way.[12] The metaphorical

10. Ibid., 134.

11. Ibid., 139.

12. Ibid.

truth, on Borg's account, beneath, through and beyond the biblical story, is valid, regardless of whether the events in the gospel narratives took place as described.

Whether there was an actual historical reality upon which the gospel writers provided elaborated resurrection accounts, as Wright contends, is, in fact, a secondary matter for Borg, of which he is highly suspicious. He posits that the "experiences of the risen Christ as a continuing presence [could have generated] . . . the story of the empty tomb."[13] In Borg's account, empathetic identification with the risen Christ leads to a profound hope, that in some ultimate sense, "the domination system [which] killed him"[14] is reversed. In the most fundamental sense this is what the resurrection signifies—"Jesus is Lord. Rome [as a symbol of the domination system] is not" and that "all the would be lords of our lives,"[15] whether personal or political, become subordinated to the lordship of Christ, onto life, onto death, and onto new life. For Wright, this great reversal is also pivotal, except for him it is deeply rooted in actual history; for without such a linkage to historical reality, the specter of denying the full significance of the incarnation would be inevitably lurking.

Unlike Wright,[16] Borg does not think the historical Jesus "foresaw his own death as a sacrifice for sin," or that he likely viewed

13. Ibid., 137.

14. Ibid.

15. Ibid., 136.

16. Wright acknowledges an atonement theology "embedded within the earliest strands of Christian tradition," though not one that focused, in its initial meaning, on the matter of individual sin and salvation. Rather, he views the sacrificial death of Christ, as first and foremost, an atonement for the sins of Israel, that "had now been dealt with," in which, in the death and resurrection of Jesus, the time of national forgiveness had arrived. Borg and Wright, *Meaning of Jesus*, 102, 103. Especially, in his more popular work, Wright does not deny the relevance of the atonement for personal salvation, but seeks to situate its individual significance in the broader narrative of Israel's story as the climax of the covenant. *Simply Christian*, 108. Critics of the "new Paul" literature express profound concerns about the limitations they perceive Wright places on the importance of individual salvation through the sacrificial blood of the risen savior. In addition to Piper, *Future of Justification*, see Johnson, "What's Wrong with

himself as Israel's Messiah. Moreover, Borg rejects any notion that "God can forgive sins only because of Jesus' sacrifice," even as he acknowledges that the sacrifice of Christ is "a powerfully true metaphor of the grace of God."[17] In Borg's view, Christ's sacrifice "is a metaphorical proclamation of the radical grace of God," pointing to "the abolition of the system of requirements, not the establishment of"[18] a new set based on a literal interpretation of a substitutionary atonement. Therefore, any notion of Jesus as God's unique son, as articulated with the highest evocation in the Gospel of John and the Epistle to the Hebrews, is viewed by Borg, as a profound and beautiful metaphor signifying the sufficiency of God's grace; one that in principle finds congruence in other stories and images reflected in other religious traditions.

Viewing the incarnation as a metaphor rather than literally descriptive of the relationship between God and Christ, Borg can claim that Christ as Lord is decisive for those affirming the Christian faith as their unique pathway to God. The claim of Christ as "the way and the truth and the life" (John 14:6) is not, however decisive in any ontological sense for adherents of other religious traditions.[19] This

---

Wright." In my view, in situating the atonement theology of Jesus of Nazareth in and for the sins of Israel, Wright provides an important bridge between the consciousness of Jesus and the theology of the mature Paul found in Romans 3:21–25, when Romans 8:19–25 and 9–11 are factored in. While such a position is invariably theoretical, through the corpus of his work, Wright has amassed a substantial case in support of it. For a supportive argument from a more theologically focused perspective, see Bauckham's, *God Crucified*, which links "the exalted and pre-existent Christ to the earthly Jesus" (45) (bold subheading removed), throughout Deutero-Isaiah (Isa 40–55), to the role of the exalted and suffering servant that Wright maintains was easily within the realm of Jesus to have internalized in his messianic calling. See Moltmann, *Way of Jesus Christ*, for a more extensive discussion of the relationship between Jesus of Nazareth and the exalted, risen Christ, along similar lines.

17. *Meaning of Jesus*, 140.

18. Ibid., 141.

19. In commenting on John 14:6, Borg, stressing its metaphorical implications, claims that "a way is a path or a road or a journey, not a set of beliefs." What was significant about Jesus is that he "embodied the way, the truth, and the life." Borg, *Reading the Bible Again for the First Time*, 211, 217. Borg contends that Jesus modeled "the way" for Christians, in a manner, in principle,

is a complex issue that requires more nuanced examination than is often given, since, in the most profound sense, this incarnational claim is based on faith rather than knowledge, yet which has the capacity to more than hold its own, apologetically against other metaphysical construals.[20] However much work is required to substantively flesh out the unique incarnational vision of God in Christ reconciling the world to himself as the foundational underpinning of the Great Tradition of Christian Orthodoxy, to shift too quickly to a "metaphorical" explanation is to slide too easily over the scandal that God is revealed most fully in a particular religious tradition, rooted in a specific time and place.

Wright

By contrast, Wright roots his theology firmly in the radical particularity of Israel's central monotheistic claim, Christologically interpreted through 1 Cor 8:6, in which there is no other greater than God in Christ reconciling the world, even as the full mystery of the biblical proclamation remains beyond human comprehension. In mirroring the power and wisdom of God in fulfilling Israel's messianic promise, Jesus, as revealed throughout the New Testament, is intimately linked with the very "Word of God" to whom "'every knee shall bow.'"[21] Wright acknowledges the lack of a fully formed incarnational theology both in the consciousness of Jesus and in the New Testament. He nonetheless insists that its roots, which were "embedded in Jewish soil,"[22] comprised the most essential theme of the earliest Christian literature. That is, "a vigorous and very early Jewish tradition took the language and mystery of Sprit, Word, Law, Presence (and/or Glory), and Wisdom and developed them in relation to Jesus of Nazareth and the Spirit."[23]

---

analogous to Buddha modeling "the way" for Buddhists.

20. For useful examples, see Craig, *Reasonable Faith* and Evans, *Historical Christ and the Jesus of Faith.*

21. *Meaning of Jesus*, 161.

22. Ibid.

23. Ibid.

It is as the climax of the covenant that Wright links Jesus' words and actions with the very presence, power, and Spirit of Israel's most holy God, in which, in its most exalted expression, Christ "and the Father are one" (John 10:30). Stated otherwise, "in Jesus of Nazareth heaven and earth have come together once and for all. The place where God's space and our space intersect and interlock is no longer the Temple of Jerusalem. It is Jesus himself."[24]

These claims call for "great risk," as Wright puts it, partly for rhetorical effect, that "our God is the true God, and your gods are worthless idols,"[25] an accusation that calls for much elaboration. In this contention, Wright is challenging the "gods of this age" (my quotes), whether "the earth goddess, Gaia, revered by some in the new age movement,"[26] the secular project of social integration via Jurgen Habermas's ideal speech act,[27] or the postmodern deconstruction of all metanarratives, except for those of its own—that all world views are historically construed, and therefore relative in their depiction of truth. Israel's God is utterly different, too, from Paul Tillich's panentheistic "'God above God,' who transcends the polarity of being and nonbeing, infinity and finitude actuality and potentiality," the "creative force that moves the world to higher possibilities,"[28] a process god.

For Wright, as well as for Borg, Christian spirituality, fully rooted in Jewish soil, is not some detached essence beyond the illusion of the body or human history. Rather, it is within the location of both the glory and limitations of human finitude where, through the veiled revelation of Israel's story, in the midst of human history, "the true God is strangely present, knowable, and lovable."[29] Within the context of who we are, both in our personal lives and public culture, the essence of Judeo-Christian spirituality remains the commandment to love the Lord God with all our

24. Wright, *Simply Christian*, 94.

25. Borg and Wright, *Meaning of Jesus*, 160.

26. Ibid., 158.

27. Habermas, *Moral Consciousness and Communicative Action*.

28. Bloesch, *God Almighty*, 21, 19.

29. Borg and Wright, *Meaning of Jesus*, 208.

heart, mind, strength and soul, and our neighbor as ourselves. It is *this* gnosis, lived through radical faith, which gives rise to increasing knowledge about that which is most important, namely, God's truth, as revealed, with special luminosity in the wisdom literature of the Old and New Testament, brought to fulfillment in the revelation of Jesus Christ.

It is with this revelation in mind that Wright embraces both creator and creation spirituality "while firmly rejecting the magical" (italics removed) aspects of the latter. Thus, "creation can be the bearer of God's presence, holiness, love, and grace,"[30] but not the source, as is at least the temptation in theologies that embrace "mother earth" as the body of God. To the extent that creation reflects God's presence, its relevance, as embodied in Judeo-Christian spirituality, is its sacramental power. So it is with history, in which for Wright, there is "no Jesus of history played off against the Christ of faith,"[31] even as the relation between history and faith requires a great deal of mediation even beyond Wright's wide-ranging knowledge and amplitude of mind.

The more fundamental point is that the essence of who Jesus is lies in the totality of what this "no other name" (my quotes) represents, through whom true God is most fully mediated. It is this that Wright insists upon—which his historical studies have helped him to confirm—much more unequivocally than does Borg. For Wright, the essence of Judeo-Christian spirituality lies in the dynamic tension between loving the world to the point of radical commitment toward its reconciliation with God and rejecting any deification of the world, and certainly its evil, which requires an element of radical separation. A "Christian spirituality, focused on and shaped by Jesus, looks at the glory and shame of it all and brings both, in prayer and liturgy before the presence of God."[32] It is this particular spirituality of "God . . . in Christ reconciling the world to himself" (2 Cor 5:19, NKJV) that speaks to the fullest aspirations and needs of humankind, in which, even as "the secret

30. Ibid., 209.

31. Ibid., 210.

32. Ibid., 212.

things belong to the Lord our God . . . the things revealed belong to us and to our children forever, that we may do all the words of this law" (Deut 29:29). Within this context of revealed truth, one finds and is found by the God who can be revered, who desires and commands our full allegiance. This is the essence of Wright's historically grounded embodied Christology.[33]

33. Selecting the Pauline passage "that God . . . [is] in Christ reconciling the world to himself " as my underlying hermeneutical framework provides space for two critical insights that do not easily converge. The first is that of interpreting the events surrounding the emergence of Christianity as synonymous with the NT depiction of the life, ministry, death, and post-resurrection sightings of Jesus of Nazareth. The second is accepting the historicity of these events without having to make definitive claims about the consciousness of Jesus or the factual accuracy of the post-crucifixion NT narratives. I agree with Wright, based on the testimony of Paul, that the early followers were gripped with the surprising revelation that Christ was raised from the dead, as attested to by the testimony of hundreds (1 Cor 15:3–8). That makes dubious claims that the resurrection sightings were the invention of the early (late first-century) church. As a non-specialist in first-century Jewish and Christian history, I accept the plausibility of Wright's conjecture that the earliest followers believed that the tomb was empty and that, based on personal testimony, they, in fact, believed Christ was raised from the dead. I can only conclude that, at the least, something of a profound nature occurred immediately surrounding the events following the crucifixion that led to the faith formation of the early followers, who staked their very lives and identity on the reality of the risen savior. Wright may be on solid ground in his claim "that the best *historical* explanation is the one which [claims] . . . [that] the tomb was indeed empty, and Jesus was indeed seen alive, because he was truly raised from the dead." Wright, *Christian Origins and the Question of God*, 3:10. Then again, events may not have proceeded in precisely that matter.

While plausible, I neither embrace nor categorically reject the prima facie case Wright makes for this argument based on the accumulated evidence, as he interprets it (an argument, to which Borg and Crossan obviously disagree), even as I admire the evidence-based rhetorical power by which he makes it. My reserve is based on a post-Enlightenment concern over explanations that require the disruption of the natural order that a literal interpretation of the various resurrection sightings seems to suggest. In raising this unease, I note that there is enough of a supernatural depiction of the resurrection sightings that move beyond an exacting literalism (Luke 24:30–32, Acts 1:6–9), toward a more mystical eucharistic vision, without denying the historicity of the described events. Clearly, something happened, in which myth, in a positive, non-pejorative sense, and historical reality were complexly intertwined, arguably, within the very mystery of God's revelation in the face of Christ (2

Cor 4:6). My concerns are not based on an acceptance of scientific reasoning as providing an exhaustive explanation, even of the natural order; my faith is grounded, in part, on the recognition that what we don't know is inexhaustibly more expansive than what we do, or can ever possibly know, even as we do know a great deal, including that of possessing persuasive, if not outright compelling, first-hand knowledge of the Christian faith.

I acknowledge that the events surrounding the life, death, and post-crucifixion reality of Jesus of Nazareth and his immediate followers were rooted in history and in the importance of the resurrection sightings for the early Christian formation of an incarnational faith. However, this is not the same thing as necessarily accepting the described events within the gospels as synonymous with that which precisely happened in the immediate post-crucifixion period. The resurrection sightings find some corroboration with Paul even if he did nothing other than reflect on the first-hand testimony of others. Paul links a burial tradition with the resurrection sightings to the earliest of believers. From this basic datum one might draw the reasonable conclusion that the full-scale empty tomb narratives emerged in the gospel narratives, which more than a few critical scholars view "as late, unhistorical accretions to the stories about the resurrection." Evans, *Historical Christ and the Jesus of Faith*, 248. For Wright, the empty tomb and the resurrection sightings, *together*, were essential for the emergence of Christianity, since on his argument, the empty tomb or resurrection sightings, alone, would have been insufficient for such a highly unexpected phenomenon. Arguing backward, from effect to cause, Wright contends that since both events were necessary for the rise of early Christianity, it can be held to a level of "high probability" that they go back to the founding era. Wright, *Christian Origins and the Question of God*, 3:706. As he further notes, "in terms of the kinds of proof which historians normally accept, the case we have presented that the tomb-plus-appearances combination is what generated early Christian belief, is as watertight as one is likely to find." Ibid., 707. Whether that is, in fact, the case is beyond what I can explore here, and, in any event, is beyond my expertise to discern. See Ibid., 706–710 for Wright's broader discussion on the importance of the two-fold sources of evidence.

The questions surrounding the time frame of these events is one of perpetual historical interest; moreover, with Wright, I agree that such questions have more than a little bearing on the nature of faith, itself, though not, as Lindbeck notes, in an ultimately "determinative" sense. *Nature of Doctrine*, 120. That is, I do not think the ultimate truth of the Christian faith depends on the historical accuracy of the gospel narratives, even as the early and continuing orthodox Christian faith tradition is intimately rooted in the historicity of the events and circumstances surrounding the life and ministry of Jesus of Nazareth, as reflected throughout the New Testament revelation. I base this claim on the assumption that both a high view of scriptural revelation and a strong connection between the Jesus of history and the Christ of faith, as a critical grounding point of an incarnational faith, can be credibly maintained,

We cannot leave things at this point without taking a closer look at the nuanced way in which the relationship between history and faith is teased out in Wright's desire to "speak truly of God."[34] Such truth, Wright notes, is a scandal in light of modern and postmodern secular thought that he seeks to counter by pointing to the presuppositional nature of all world views, while relying ultimately on faith through God's "self-revelation" via the confluence of Scripture and history. It is this, Wright claims (pace Deut. 29:29), that "has given us such knowledge as is possible and appropriate for us,"[35]

even if it cannot be precisely determined what actually transpired in the life and times of Jesus of Nazareth, particularly in the immediate post-crucifixion period. With the narrative theologians I have no difficulty in viewing the Bible as a realistic-like, revelatory genre comprised of factual and fictive depiction of events—in which there is simply insufficient evidence to discern anything like their exact mix—through which God worked in and through the historical Jesus to reconcile the world. How the Christian revelation emerged in the immediacy of time and place within the first half of the first century, remains, in many respects, unknown, in which we have testimony that points to a mystery, where, in the full revelation, when "God . . . [will] be all in all" (1 Cor 15:28b), "the perishable" will "clothe itself with the imperishable, and the mortal with immortality" (1 Cor 15:53–54). At that time, in the ultimate unveiling, death will be swallowed up through "the victory . . . [of] our Lord Jesus Christ" (1 Cor 15:57). Echoing this Pauline hope, I view the resurrection narratives, at the very least, as a sign of the most profound sort, of that victory. They may be more than that, including the possibility of closely resembling that which actually happened in real time and place. Intuitively, I am led to conclude that there had to be a close correspondence of some sort between events as narrated and events as lived; nonetheless, one that can only be grasped through the mystery of God's revelation in and through Christ, in which faith can be perceived only as "the substance of things hoped for, the evidence of things not seen" (Heb 11:1). Because of the gap, I do not base my faith on the prospect of an exact correspondence, however plausible, or not, that likelihood may be, but on the belief that God is reconciling the world to himself through the teaching, healing, crucifixion, and resurrection of Christ, in his capacity as the Jesus of history and the living Lord of all creation.

> Oh, the depth and riches of the wisdom and knowledge of God. How unsearchable his judgments, and his paths beyond tracing out. Who has known the mind of the Lord? Or who has been his counselor? Who has ever given to God, that God should repay them? For from him and through him and for him are all things. To him be the glory forever. Amen (Rom 11:33–36).

34. Borg and Wright, *Meaning of Jesus*, 214.

35. Ibid.

even without the capacity to unravel all mysteries in the quest to transcend human fallibility and finitude, the underlying temptation of Gnosticism. Within this framework Wright constructs a methodology that combines building best case hypotheses and juxtaposing them in light of the perceived limitations of other perspectives. It is this "critical realism" that grounds his analysis of the interdependent relationship between faith and history, where to "split the historical Jesus off from the Christ known in faith, as some have tried to do [including certain narrative theologians], and you are left without a revelation of the one true God within our world, the world of physicality and history."

As a historically-based religion that claims to embody the fullness of God in its founder, it matters whether there is a solid correspondence between what is stated in the written testimonies and what actually happened, in fact, even as the quest for the historical Jesus remains ever elusive in the most fundamental details. Working from an epistemology based on critical realism, Wright acknowledges that "whether the [gospel] stories really did happened" is beyond the purview of contemporary historical evidence to discern, even as the critical point remains that "everyone who told them thought they did."[36]

The question remains not whether, but how faith and history interact, for without question, as Wright has so magnificently illustrated, the origins of Christianity were embedded in the dynamic culture of Second Temple Judaism and the personage of Jesus of Nazareth and his early followers. What Wright says bears careful observation, for in the final analysis he acknowledges the invariable gaps in the historical record that limit what can be definitively claimed, even as there may be highly credible evidence to draw upon for best case hypothesis formation. Rejecting Borg's characterization of "history metaphorized" in pushing the New Testament to signify meaning beyond authorial intent, one of Wright's central points is that the gospel "authors *thought* [italics added] the

36. Ibid. 216.

events they were recording—all of them, not just some—actually happened."[37]

Noting that they could have been mistaken about, say the resurrection sightings or the transfiguration story, Wright argues that if that were the case the gospel writers would have failed "to convey the most important meaning they had in mind, which was precisely in these events *as historical events* Israel's God, the world's creator, had acted decisively and climactically within creation within Israel's history."[38] As a historically-based religion that claims to embody the fullness of God in its founder, it matters whether there is solid correspondence between what is stated in the written testimonies and what actually happened, in fact, even as the quest for the historical Jesus remains ever elusive in the most fundamental details.[39]

Wright is closely parsing matters. It is one thing to say that the Bible speaks of truths that are "dependent on history," and even to argue that events, as described, have a solid plausibility as to their facticity. It is another altogether to claim that what is written in the gospels is an accurate description of what actually happened, a position which Wright does not claim, though he seems to beg the question then of precisely "what Israel's God was doing in *actual history*."[40]

---

37. Ibid., 215.

38. Ibid.

39. Evans asserts that in "affirming the importance of the historicity of the incarnational narrative, Christians affirm both that it is important that the events which the narrative depict actually occurred, and that we have some means of becoming acquainted with the narrative or believing that the events thereby depicted occurred." *The Historical Christ and the Jesus of Faith*, 12. This is a position closely analogous to that of Wright. The issue remains how close the correspondence is between the various gospel and Pauline claims of the risen Christ and what actually transpired during the life of Jesus and the immediate post-crucifixion events attributed to him and his disciples, and how much it matters to a vibrant Christian faith. Evans and Wright explore these concerns in considerable nuance and depth, however ultimately inconclusive their analyses remain.

40. Borg and Wright, *Meaning of Jesus*, 215.

In light of the cloud of witnesses that attested to the resurrection sightings, Wright draws as the most likely conclusion that the narrated events on the road to Emmaus and elsewhere actually did happen. For if they did not it would raise the profoundest questions about any such claims having a historical referent as the basis in identifying the universal God in the radical particularity of Israel's truth, in its ultimately revealed form in the messiahship of Jesus of Nazareth. The full force of Wright's embodied Christology depends, then, on the accuracy of an actual historical event, namely, the bodily resurrection of Jesus from the dead, as documented in all of the gospels, with supportive evidence from the letters of Paul, given, even, the likely elaboration in some of the gospel narratives.

What Wright does not sufficiently discuss in *The Meaning of Jesus* is the difference between history as lived and the realistically-based historical description as a biblical genre, which includes both history as lived and history as remembered. Closely related is history posited in the mouth of Jesus in the manner of the ancient historian who sought through narrative to highlight the essence of the historical character through descriptions that were invariably idealistic (especially in John, but in all of the gospel portrayals), however true to the character and to the era portrayed. Still, with Wright, Paul's writings provide more than a little persuasive evidence that the tradition canonized in the gospels formed very early, even as the first several years after the crucifixion remain opaque to precise historical description. In short, Wright has provided tantalizing insights on the relationship between faith and history, even as the questions he raises beg additional ones that require further investigation.

5

Concluding Reflections

Borg and Wright Revisited

GIVEN THE BOOK'S DIALOGICAL form, its accessibility to critically-informed lay persons, and its wide use among adult church study groups, *The Meaning of Jesus: Two Visions* is a useful text in highlighting theological tensions in contemporary Protestantism, particularly along the mainline-evangelical theological axis. While it remains only an introduction to the vast work of Borg and Wright, *The Meaning of Jesus* opens up a broad range of issues accessible to the laity and clergy, alike. Readers can derive valuable insights from the text through individual reading, group study, and dialogue across denominational and theological boundaries. The role of metaphor and myth, the importance of historical accuracy as a signpost for theological truth, the inclusive/exclusive debate on the relationship between Christianity and other world religions, and ultimately the basis and shape of Christian belief are examined through divergent and sometimes complementary perspectives that our two authors open up.

Given the core premise underlying my theology of viewing the Bible in its comprehensive breadth as the interpretive basis to engage the culture through the prism of what theologians refer to as the Great Tradition of Christian orthodoxy,[1] Borg's theological liberalism has largely served as my foil. This is not to discount Borg's project of seeking to make Christianity viable to contemporary Christians. Nor is it to disregard his influence in assisting those many persons for whom the traditional orthodox story is no longer (or never seemed) persuasive in opening up renewed faith possibilities by envisioning both the Bible and Jesus with fresh eyes. Borg has presented a credible picture of Christianity as a beautiful and profound pathway to the holy, one in which those who choose to do so can enter in and find rich meaning without having to diminish the salvationist possibility of other religious traditions and faith journeys. I accept the intent of Borg's apologetic project, even though I think it preferable to assist those who are on the periphery to better understand the core doctrines of the faith in ways they can assimilate in forming a generously orthodox Christian identity.[2]

While expressing qualified empathy for Borg's intent, I have problems with several of his assumptions. Specifically, I wonder the extent to which his metaphorical interpretation is Christian to its core, as opposed to exhibiting a profound Christian sensibility within a syncretistic context. I raise this concern based on his claim that all of the world religions are, more or less, equally valid as representing divergent pathways to ultimately the same underlying truth, as reflected through the various traditions and "metaphors" upon which they are constructed. In accordance with

1. Demetrion, *In Quest of a Vital Protestant Center*.

2. Based on my own engagement with the various essays of Walter Brueggemann, I can appreciate Borg's desire to convey something of the depth and beauty of the Christian faith to those on the periphery of the Christian orthodox tradition. For those more inclined to embrace, or at least, to give serious consideration to the fundamental doctrines of the Great Tradition of Christian orthodoxy, the thirty week, *Christian Believer* study, authored and edited by Ellsworth Kalas, is one valuable resource. The study consists of a book of primary source readings that include a diversity of views spanning the centuries and theological traditions on each core doctrine, a theologically oriented study manual that includes application activities, and a DVD set narrated by the noted church historian Justo Gonzalez.

the broad stream of orthodox Christian theology, I take as axiomatic that it is God, the father, that is revealed in Jesus Christ, as God's unique son, and that the Bible, in its comprehensive depth and breadth, is the primary (though not exclusive) source of revelation, which requires the illumination of the Holy Spirit to even partially internalize. At the center of the orthodox tradition is this incarnational orientation which drives the assumption that God is revealed most fully and truly in and through Christ, not simply as an existential faith-based experience, but as an ontological truth claim with universal applicability, however limited our knowledge may be of such matters, which by its very nature, transcends human capacity to fully grasp.

This perspective does not discount the value of other viewpoints, religious or secular, but it does contend that, in the most fundamental sense, the fullest revelation of God given to humankind is reflected in Christianity, even as there is much to learn and potentially to incorporate from other religions and secular world views.[3] Given the limitations of one's own knowledge, as well as a healthy regard for the views of others, humility requires openness to other constructions of reality. However, one can only go so far in embracing the pluralism of ideas and beliefs without sacrificing that which is most essential; namely, the belief that Christ is the way, the truth, and the life, ultimately, without equivocation, doubt notwithstanding, in which the pathway of syncretism is nothing short of idolatry. Granted, this can sound extremely arrogant, which, when embraced as a form of triumphalism, contains its own idolatrous temptations. It is a scandal of major proportions. That notwithstanding, I accept the core orthodox tenets that the grounding points of Christianity are embodied in the sovereignty of God, the incarnation, the Trinity, the atonement, and the central role of the Bible in its canonical breadth and depth as the primary source of Christian revelation. Based on these premises, God revealed in his fullest and truest sense can be through no other name than the Word made flesh, lest one surrender the very essence of faith to that which might be viewed,

3. Yong, *Dialogical Spirit.*

evangelistically, as the idolatry of syncretism in the name of religious globalism.[4] This is my first hypothesis.

A most related one is that any substantive revitalization of mainline Protestantism will require a return to a fully-orbed and "generous" orthodox position, thoroughly conversant with modern culture and scholarship; one based upon a renewal and reinvigoration of its own religious traditions.[5] Among other things, such renewal would include in-depth Bible study and biblically-based worship through which the ultimate vocabulary and meaning of the faith would be grounded, in which scriptural revelation, in its canonical and hermeneutical comprehensiveness, would become the primary source for the formation of Christian identity within congregational settings and seminary halls. I encourage those sympathetic to Borg's project to further flesh out their assumptions and the implications thereof. However, the pathway of Borg, and more broadly, the Jesus Seminar, is not the tack I am taking here, as I am working from a more orthodox perspective and seek to build my case from within a broad-based evangelical-Reformed hermeneutical sensibility that reaches toward extensive ecumenical comprehensiveness.[6]

The critical topic with which I seek to grapple is the role of history in its relationship to faith. My primary focus has been on divergent interpretations of the historical Jesus and the significance thereof of the Christ of faith, as reflected in the views of Borg and Wright. I will not recount that discussion here, except to allude back to the ways in which the authors' Christologies are invariably informed by their interpretations of this history. As a faith grounded in both Jewish tradition and the broader ancient world, it is impossible to grasp something of the origins of Christianity without acknowledging the importance of this history. It is in and

4. For an insightful discussion of the claims of Christian particularity based on the revelation of Christ grounded in the doctrines of the incarnation, see Evans, *Historical Christ and the Jesus of Faith*, 98–136.

5. Newbigin addresses these matters with keen insight in *Foolishness to the Greeks* and *Gospel in a Pluralistic Age*.

6. Bloesch, *A Theology of Word and Spirit*, Fackre, *Ecumenical Faith in Evangelical Perspective*, and Demetrion, *In Quest of a Vital Protestant Center*.

through these ancient traditions that the monotheistic Lord God revealed himself to humankind. This is the scandal of particularity that proponents of religious globalism categorically reject, upon which the core claims of Christianity are firmly rooted. What is awesome in the magisterial sense is less why God has chosen this particular pathway through Israel's history—a question that in the final analysis cannot be answered by human beings—than *how* God has revealed himself through this tradition and the nature of his character and the core precepts that "belong to us and to our children forever" (Deut 29:29b). The particularistic contention of this faith tradition cannot be proven; it can only be lived, illustrated, and compared to other world constructions. Nonetheless, it grounds the axiomatic presuppositions of orthodox Christianity and gives shape to its foundational doctrinal vocabulary, to which, in the final analysis, apologetics is subordinate—faith, the substance of things hoped for, the evidence of things not seen. At its bottom, this faith is a self-authenticating one, based, arguably, on substantial testimonial and documentary evidence, but not grounded in irrefutable proof. Few things are.

There is another sense in which history is at work—the contemporary understanding of religious studies as an academic discipline. Not only Christianity, but all the world's religions are rooted in specific times and places. Those that have endured have evolved through culture and history, which has invariably shaped their emergent manifestations through the centuries. These obvious truths have impacted the study of contemporary religion in such academic disciplines as sociology, history, and anthropology, primarily through a comparative approach which eliminates the religious—including the academic discipline of theological reflection—as a legitimate source of knowledge in its own right. Such assumptions are grounded in a secularized world view that posits the religious in the realm of "belief," beyond rational knowledge or communication. This "self-evident" secularized world view is not only pervasive within the academy, but within large sectors of Western culture.[7]

7. Taylor, *Secular Age*, esp. 423–593.

Any revitalization of mainline Protestantism will need to grapple with these academic norms and the broader cultural paradigms which reinforce them while radically challenging the hegemony of secularization based on its own articulated framework, grounded in the precept that God in Christ is reconciling the world to himself. This counterclaim needs to be made on reasons that can be defended, in principle, academically, in a manner that resonates within the context of common public discourse, in which the religious is neither privileged nor marginalized. The challenge of bringing the religious to the public square in a manner that honors and defends its own core assumptions without magisterially imposing them on those who do not accept them, or deliberately marginalizing them, for that matter, by categorically ruling them out of bounds, will require a subtle combination of courage and discernment.[8] Such a prospect will require an expansion of the academic canon in a manner broadly analogous to the emergence of gender and ethnic studies in the recognition of new epistemological categories in the engagement of scholarly discourse. Over the past century, Protestant mainline theology has made a major contribution in seeking to correlate religious categories within the context of modern cultural and intellectual presuppositions.

That is important work, but only half the story. The other part is to probe the underlying values of the culture—in our case, Western culture—through the theological presuppositions of what C. S. Lewis refers to as "mere Christianity" and to make the religious as intellectually viable as other human disciplines of knowledge building. Without this shift—the category of God acting in history, revealed, in a most significant, though partially, allusive manner through Scripture—any such project cannot be even credibly posited. This revelatory hypothesis of God in Christ reconciling the world may be viewed as an incredulous proposition, a scandal which Christian scholarship needs to bring to the academy in light

8. Marsden, *Soul of the American University*. For a more technical study that critically engages the academic disciplines of philosophy, history, and theology in a manner that could be construed as interdisciplinary, see Evans, *Historical Christ and the Jesus of Faith*.

of other truth claims that mightily contend for influence on their own persuasive powers of legitimacy. Without this prospect, studies of the historical Jesus can only be stymied by secular presuppositions taken as axiomatic, in which historicism, more broadly, culture, is viewed as the "center of value" of human meaning, the interpretive grid upon which the academic study of religion is currently based.[9]

What I am countering with is God embodied in Christ. As a truth claim, even as its articulation can only be offered as a hypothetical construct. It is this particular scandal, based on its own epistemological sources of evidence, which radical Christianity is compelled to defend with all the subtlety, depth, and humility that its advocates can muster, without which the very basis of faith, short of some syncretistic substitution, disintegrates. To the extent that scholarly Christian interpretation is repressed as a legitimate voice in the broader academic discourse community, such studies are invariably flawed in categorically rejecting the epistemology of faith as a viable basis of informed knowledge construction on its own terms.[10] Such faith, in search of greater knowledge presupposes the reality of God, in which, as in any disciplined body of study, ontological truth claims overshoot a knower's epistemological grasp.[11]

9. Olson, in *Journey of Modern* Theology, referencing Ernst Troeltsch, summarizes this position as follows: "On the one hand the believer ventures to have faith in Jesus Christ; on the other hand the believer ought to acknowledge that historical research can never prove this faith valid and that, in fact, the object of faith is itself, himself (Jesus), historically relative and not absolute." Ibid., 180. According to Trolesch—and a wide range of liberal biblical and religious scholars, including Borg—all *knowledge* upon which the Christian faith is based can only be established on such historicist presuppositions. See ibid. (167–90) for a comprehensive overview of Troeltsch and the influence of historicism on his study of the Christian religion. On value prioritization, see Niebuhr, "Center of Value."

10. This issue is explored with much discernment in Evans, *Historical Christ and the Jesus of Faith*. See Craig, *Reasonable Faith*, for a similar argument from a more distinctively evangelical perspective.

11. For a useful discussion on various supernaturalist and naturalist interpretations of the relationship between Christ and culture within Christian historiography, see, Clary, "Evangelical Historiography."

One of the major consequences of the scholarship on the historical Jesus over the past one-hundred-and-fifty years is the emphasis on the constructed nature of Jesus as a literary artifact of the early church, which, while grounded in some history, can be viewed as an ideal portrait with ideological intent.[12] This has resulted in much skepticism, particularly in mainline congregations, of the basic truth claims of the New Testament. The critical research stemming from the academic disciplines of history and literary theory have generated considerable fundamentalist and evangelical reaction in the insistence in many quarters of claims of scriptural inerrancy, a position which is categorically rejected in some rather different ways within liberal and neo-orthodox Protestantism.[13]

Borg's embrace of faith beyond history has its own problems, particularly when linked to his pluralistic assumptions that religious traditions are metaphorical expressions for truths that are ultimately inexpressible through language. This posture denies the fundamental contention that Christ—as revealed, especially, in John, Colossians, Hebrews, portions of the two Corinthian letters, and Romans—*is* the unique Incarnation of God in human flesh without remainder or qualification, the core presupposition of orthodox Christianity, however much the mystery of this claim is ultimately a doxological- rather than a fully grounded knowledge-based one. Seeking to turn over a century of scholarship on its head, Wright rejects the notion of a great divide between the Jesus of history and the Christ of faith. In his massive project spanning several thick scholarly and a variety of more popular books, Wright seeks to demonstrate that there is much more continuity than generally assumed between what the historical evidence discloses and the claims of the gospels and the letters of Paul. In their respective ways, Borg and Wright have done much to deepen the discussion on the relationship between faith and history. Still, on both sides of the equation, problems abound.

Concerns with Borg's interpretation of the ultimate significance of Jesus' message and ministry as residing beyond the

12. Wright, *Contemporary Quest for Jesus*, 1–28.
13. Pinnock, *Biblical Revelation*, esp. 162–74.

New Testament depiction and Second Temple Judaism have been noted. The issue I take with Wright is not whether God acts in and through history, but how. It is one thing to say that the basis of the Christian revelation was rooted in actual historical events. It is another altogether to assert that those historical events were more or less synonymous with the events described in the New Testament. I take as given that there was an intrinsic relationship of some significant sort, in both the pre- and post-crucifixion, period between what actually happened and what emerged in the gospel narratives. Notwithstanding the vast scholarship on this topic, including Wright's massive research, there is much about their correlation that remains unknown. The preponderance of evidence may point to a great deal of continuity, as Wright maintains, between the gospel descriptions, including the resurrection sightings, and what transpired in the historical life of Jesus of Nazareth and his followers, both before and immediately after Calvary. Then again, the discontinuity between the NT description and the actual events may be considerably wider than he is willing to acknowledge.

The matter might be less problematic if in fact, Wright's major contentions could be conclusively settled.[14] Even there, the temptation would remain that of drawing on history too much to substantiate the claims of orthodox Christianity on the core apostolic essentials rather than relying on faith, itself, as the substance of things hoped for. On faith's grounding point in "the Spirit who raised . . . Christ from the dead" (Rom 8:11) as the ultimate basis for belief—including the possibility that the primary source of revelation is based on a realistic-like biblical narrative that contains fictive and non-fictive elements—the disciplines of history and other naturalistic modes of knowledge, such as science, philosophy, and literary studies provide supplemental resources, more or less reliable and more or less essential, in any given context.[15]

14. In addition to the various cited texts of Borg, see also Crossan, *Jesus* and *Historical Jesus* for perspectives highly critical of Wright's claims on the underlying continuity between the Jesus of history and the Christ of faith.

15. See Evans, *Historical Christ and the Jesus of Faith*, 283–301 for a useful discussion on the complementary interaction between internal (self-authenticating) and external evidentiary sources of faith. On the relationship between

The question posed rhetorically to Wright is the location of faith if Borg and Crossan are even partially accurate in their core assumptions, particularly on their interpretations of the resurrection narratives. Wright may be correct in his postulation that the resurrection accounts given in the gospels have a substantive basis in what really happened, a position for which he has argued with much cogency against scholarly perspectives that reject this view.[16] Wright also notes that our knowledge of the period between 30–40 CE remains scant, in which historians really cannot say for sure what took place around the events surrounding the stories of the empty tomb and the resurrection sightings.[17] Historical analysis is useful; more forcefully, essential if Christianity is to move out of the catacombs. Nonetheless, such knowledge as its study can provide, while valuable, remains, ultimately, limited in terms of

---

"historicized fiction" and "fictionalized history" (ibid., 61) applied to biblical hermeneutics, see Long, *Art of Biblical History*, 58–87, for a useful discussion. Long puts his interpretive emphasis on the latter term, noting the importance of "*artistry* or *craft*" (ibid., 62), designed to highlight the significance of particular passages where the biblical text makes historical claims. Long provides important qualifying considerations against moving to a too easy polarity between factual and fictive interpretations of biblical texts. However, in my view, he too readily dismisses the importance that Dorrien, Lindbeck, and other postliberal theologians place in viewing the descriptive portions of the Bible through the prism of a realistic-like narrative, wherein factual and fictive elements that comprise a given text are not easily susceptible to definitive delineation.

16. Wright, *Christian Origins and the Question of God*, 3, esp. 685–718.

17. Based upon the presupposition that the "detailed passion accounts . . . [are] not [a form of] *history remembered but prophecy historicized*," (*Jesus*, 145), Crossan argues that the body of Jesus was never taken away by Joseph of Arimathea. Rather, Crossan speculates that Jesus was buried in a "shallow grave," in which his body was likely devoured by "scavenging dogs." Moreover, this Joseph, as described in the gospels, as both "'a respected member of the council' . . . and also 'waiting expectantly for the kingdom of God,'" was likely a literary construct to provide "exactly what" the gospel writers "needed to turn a vague hope that *they* would have buried him into a specific and definite event." Ibid., 156. I do not suggest that Crossan is correct. I simply make the more modest statement that the issues surrounding the historical accuracy of the various events surrounding the gospel narratives, while important in their penultimate significance, are far from conclusively resolved.

authenticating the fundamental matters related to "the faith . . . once for all delivered to the saints" (Jude 3, KJV); one grounded in history—as both lived and remembered—rooted within the deeper mystery of God's revelation (Deut 29:29a).

The Incarnate and Inscripturated Word as True Mystery

For my own view, I build on J. I. Packer, Lesslie Newbigin, Gabriel Fackre, and others, who, in their different ways, maintain that the ultimate source of reliability is the revelation of God, as witnessed throughout the entire Bible via its many genres. Any such appropriation of this truth claim, which requires the indwelling power of the Holy Spirit to internalize, necessitates subtle interpretation and critical exegesis with the support of tradition, common, critical, and canonical sense, and all the tools of modern scholarship that may be available.[18] In conjunction with a broad stream of evangelical and postliberal narrative theologians, I argue that the various contexts that impinge on biblical and theological interpretation are ultimately ministerial to the magisterial grounding point of biblical revelation. Following Packer, it is "God unchanging" that provides the critical linchpin in linking history and faith, as revealed most fully, in and through Scripture. Packer notes the wide historical gulf between the biblical era and our own, in which the Bible may be viewed as "intensely interesting," while "seem[ing] very far away." He observes, from the perspective of history and culture, the Bible "belongs to *that* world not to *this* world."[19]

This distance between the biblical world and our own has the potential of reinforcing among many churchgoers and ministers a spectral view of the Bible as largely irrelevant to the conditions and issues confronting the modern world, in which, at its best, its "stories" provide a paradigmatic glimpse into the profound recesses of the human condition. This is far from unimportant work.

18. Fackre discusses these different aspects of biblical interpretation in *Christian Story*, 2, 157–210.

19. Packer, *Knowing God*, 76.

However, it remains insufficient for a more thoroughly canonical appreciation of the Bible if the perspective of the Great Tradition[20] is to flourish in both mainline and evangelical congregations, without which there remains something fundamentally askew.

Packer's core argument is that the link between the biblical text and us is not to be found at the level of history and culture. Rather, "the link is God himself," in which the God that the biblical writers expounded upon and worshiped is the same God that speaks to us, however differently, from the biblical era to the contemporary period.[21] This mystery-grounded faith in the eternal presence of the living God is revealed through the course of the inspired biblical text via what Fackre refers to as "an overarching narrative [from creation to consummation] that renders the identity of the Christian God." From this vantage point, "Jesus

---

20. On the importance of the "Great Tradition" of Christian orthodoxy, which includes vital streams from Eastern Orthodox and Roman Catholic perspectives, see Sherman, *Revitalizing Theological Epistemology*, 129, 131,141, and 142, and 241. As Sherman notes, Great Tradition Christians include postconservative evangelicals who, while viewing the Bible as the primary and indispensable source of faith and revelation, draw broadly from the wide stream of ecumenical resources in placing a significant emphasis on the importance of the Holy Spirit and the ecumenical church in its historical and contemporary expressions. Writing from a more traditional evangelical perspective in his seven-volume Christian Foundations series, Bloesch has also expanded his theological scope in this manner. This is noted by Dorrien, in *Remaking Evangelical Theology*, who links Bloesch "to a group of 'Great Tradition' evangelicals who are clearly more interested in pursuing dialogue with conservative Catholic and Orthodox theologians than with progressive [postconservative] evangelicals." Ibid., 193. As noted by Sherman, *in Revitalizing Theological Epistemology* 131, an appreciation of the Great Tradition crosses significant theological boundaries in the quest for more holistic hermeneutical approaches to the core doctrines and practices of the Christian faith, while maintaining the centrality the Bible as the ultimate grounding point of faith.

21. Packer, *Knowing God*, 77. Elsewhere, Packer notes, "just as it is possible to identify in all the books of Scripture universal and abiding truths about the will, work, and ways of God, it is equally possible to find in every one of them universal and abiding principles of loyalty and devotion to the holy, gracious, Creator; and then to detach these from the particular situations to which, and within which, the books apply them, and then to reapply them to ourselves in the places, circumstances, and conditions of our own lives today." Packer, "Understanding the Bible," 147.

Christ," revealed most fully in and through the New Testament, is "the interpretive key to the whole narrative."[22] From a similar angle, Grenz and Franke note, "the Spirit leads us to view ourselves and all reality in light of an unabashedly Christian and specifically biblical interpretive framework so that we might thereby understand and respond to the challenges of life in the present as the contemporary embodiment of a faith community that spans the ages."[23] This perspective is shared by evangelical and postliberal theologians, alike,[24] such as Gary Dorrien, even as traditional evangelicals, such as Packer, take issue with Dorrien's disparagement of the doctrine of biblical inerrancy and his Barth-influenced "post-modern dialectic of Word and Spirit" through which he characterizes Christianity as "true myth."[25] As Dorrien

22. Fackre, *Doctrine of Revelation*, 5.

23. Grenz and Franke, *Beyond Foundationalism*, 81.

24. Phillips and Okholm. eds., *Nature of Confession.*

25. In *Word as True Myth*, Dorrien takes issue with any interpretation that maintains that "Christianity cannot be mythical and true." Ibid., 231. As he notes, "there is no compelling reason for Christianity to oversell the distinctive or antimythical character of Christianity, for the gospel uses and is an example of mythical speech. As Barth told Bultmann, 'there is no need for us to have a guilty conscience' about recognizing and *proclaiming* the gospel in all of its mythical character, for if all of the myth in the gospel were removed, it would be impossible to witness to Christ. Whether it is called myth, or saga, mythical speech is intrinsic to Christianity. If Christianity is true, it is true as true myth." Ibid., 236.

An analysis of the important distinctions between traditional and post-conservative evangelical, and postliberal theology, as reflected in the work of Packer, Fackre, Grenz and Franke, and Dorrien, on the extent to which the New Testament is historically factual in its substantive claims, extends beyond the scope of this discussion. The critical point that I raise here is their mutual adherence (even with their substantial differences in emphasis) to a theology of Word and Spirit as the magisterial source of Christian revelation that is ultimately more foundational than the academic discipline of history and the liberal emphasis within critical biblical studies over the past one-hundred-and-fifty years. This is not to discount the important *ministerial* role of such modes of scholarship as history, literary studies, and philosophy in deepening faith's understanding, as reflected, in their different, and occasionally complementary ways, in the work of Borg and Wright on the historicity of Jesus and its relationship to the Christ of faith.

Perhaps there is need for a fourth quest for the historical Jesus grounded in

further notes, "all of our efforts to express the actuality behind the Christ event are less true than the [mysterious] actuality," itself, in which "the images that become God's truth acquire this status . . . only through grace." Through such a revelation, the true essence of "God remains [partially] hidden from us."[26] Such veiled revelation, which is given to us in the face of Christ, includes "the various images that scripture contains, which, through the movement of God's illuminative Word . . . can become God's truth"[27] for us.

Whatever one may make of Dorrien's Barth-like appropriation of the Word, it is this hermeneutical dynamic via the work of the Holy Spirit through the illumination of fallible, finite, historically conditioned human beings that bridges the gap: God speaking in and through the entirety of Scripture, from the initial writers to readers across the centuries, from cultures of origin to cultures of reception around the world. It is this biblical text through which God "condescends to employ human language"[28] that Packer and others view as utterly trustworthy, however limited our own un-

---

the Christ of faith as the starting point of investigation, which can account for the important work of previous scholars, while shifting the quest to another set of questions and presuppositions. Dorrien provides a useful summary statement for such an orienting framework: "The Word made flesh is the first and definitive sign of all signs, but the Word is made known to us only after the flesh, through the Spirit. For in Christ we see the human face of God no longer according to the flesh, but in and through the movement of the Spirit." *Word as True Myth*, 239. In this—in conjunction with revelatory significance of the entirety of the biblical canon, it should be added—we are given a sign of God in Christ reconciling the world to himself. There would be much merit to ground a renewed quest in such a premise and to work from there to search out historical connections. Wright's work provides some important pointers. However, in my view, he places too much reliance on the prospect of the historical accuracy of the synoptic gospels, a topic that would have only antiquarian interest without the revelation of God in Christ that places the incarnation, at least for the Christian community, as the central topic of focus. Such a project can be only described as theologically grounded historical analysis, in which the biblical perspective is the basis for the determination of what is of ultimate significance in the historical sphere.

26. Ibid., 238, 239.

27. Ibid., 239.

28. Packer, *Knowing and Doing the Will of God*, 45.

derstanding remains. The Word—in its most encapsulated form, as God in Christ reconciling the world to himself—revealed, in and through scripturally based inspiration, meditation, and faith unrelenting in the midst, even, of the most profound questioning, and ultimately grace, is the surer grounding of Christian belief. It is this Word, as the crystalized pinnacle of the New Testament revelation, that is none other than God, himself, "who was with God" since the beginning of creation (John 1:1–2). "In him was life, and that life was the life of all mankind" (John 1:4).

> To all who did receive him, to those who believed in his name, he gave the right to become children of God—children born not of natural descent, nor of human decision or a husband's will, but born of God. The Word became flesh and made his dwelling among us. We have seen his glory, the glory of the, one and only Son, who came from the Father, full of grace and truth (John 1:12–14).

History, philosophy, science, and other interpretative modalities in search of knowledge can, and often need to be drawn upon in a supplementary manner. It is, however, a return to and a rediscovery of a richer theology of Scripture and the Great Tradition of Christian orthodoxy which I am advocating as a central pathway to mainline renewal through constructive dialogue with centrist evangelicals—one that echoes the intent, if not the approach, of Borg and Wright in their discussion of the relationship between the historical Jesus and the Christ of faith.

As discussed throughout this book, the historical events surrounding the life and ministry of Jesus of Nazareth retain a central place for an incarnational faith, yet one that cannot be separated from the mystery of God's revelation, as embodied in the gospel narratives of what C. S. Lewis refers to as mythical, in their most fundamental storied forms. Viewed in its most positive sense, myth, according to Lewis, mediates the gap between reality (what Dorrien refers to as "actuality") and our interpretation of it. In this, myth has a universal function through which our understanding of Christianity (as true myth) gains much by being processed as such, by taking into account our imaginations and emotions as well as our minds. In Lewis's terms, "the heart of Christianity is a myth which is also a fact,"[29] however much a determination of what the facts are at the heart of the matter may not be as clear cut as Lewis surmised.[30] As an imaginative pathway bridging direct experience—which we cannot get outside of without dissolving *that* experience—and conceptualization, myth is not so much a pointer "to truth, but [to] reality," a reality that for Lewis is found, in its most complete form, in the incarnation, which transcends myth in a similar way that "myth transcends thought."[31]

To be sure, this is a most peculiar myth, radically different from that of Gnosticism, in which, in the words of Hans Frei, "the savior is complexly identified with a specific human being, Jesus of Nazareth."[32] In his contrast with Gnosticism, Frei rejects the use of myth, in its "out of [historical] time,"[33] portrayal of Christ. For Frei, Jesus can only be rightly understood in and through the gospels, in their realistic-like, *in historical time*, presentations, which he distinguishes from history, as such, as sifted through the canon of contemporary historiography, without denying the historicity of the gospel resurrection narratives.

In bringing Frei's views into this discussion, I am using the term, myth, in a broader sense than his usage, as does Dorrien and Lewis, in visualizing something of the mystery of God's unveiling in Christ that language can only partially convey that is, nonetheless carried, through the storied narrative of the biblical revelation. Particularly for Lewis, the Christian story is mediated through all the resources of the literary imagination even in its history-like presentation. Such an understanding fuses the ineffable—more

29. "Myth Becomes Fact," 41.

30. The alternative that Lewis posed in *Mere Christianity*, of whether Jesus of Nazareth was, and knew himself to be "the Son of God," "or else a madman, or something worse"(52), presupposes that the gospel narratives were synonymous with the actual historical events. As discussed throughout this book, this is a matter of much contestability in the scholarly literature on the historical Jesus.

31. "Myth Becomes Fact," 41.

32. Frei, *Identity of Jesus Christ*, loc. 1865.

33. Ibid., loc. 1876.

pointedly, the transcendent—that permeates the resurrection narratives, which surpasses human comprehension, with the "singular, unsubstitutable, and self-focused being"[34] of Jesus Christ, exhibited throughout those narratives and the entirety of the gospel depictions. As Frei further explains, "the Christian savior story is that of [the unique presence and identify of] Jesus himself . . . . [as] the crucial person in the story." In contrast to gnostic depictions, "his identity is not grasped by a knowledge of savior *stories* [italics added], including those which appropriated his figure to represent them,"[35] but only in the unique characterization of the gospel narratives and the utterly irreplaceable identity and presence of Jesus as exhibited in them. As Lewis describes it:

> The old myth of the dying god, *without ceasing to be myth* comes down from the heaven of legend and imagination to the earth of history. It *happens*—at a particular date, in a particular place, followed by definable historical consequences. We pass from a Bader or an Osiris, dying nobody knows when or where, to a historical person crucified . . . under Pontius Pilate. By becoming fact it does not cease to be myth. That is the miracle.[36]

The fact that the most central aspects of the post-crucifixion portrayals remain closed to verifiable historical documentation lends to the gospel portrayals, particularly of the empty tomb and resurrection sightings, a mythopoeic dimension that reinforces a literary perspective of envisaging them as realistic-like narratives through which the mystery of the incarnation is embodied.[37] "Confronted by the claim that Jesus Christ rose from the dead,"

34. Ibid., loc. 1898.

35. Ibid.

36. "Myth Becomes Fact," 41. As he further states, "to be truly Christian we must both assent to the historical fact [of the Christian revelation in its totality] and also receive [it as] . . . myth (fact though it has become) with the same imaginative embrace which we accord to all myths. The one is hardly more necessary than the other." Ibid., 41–42.

37. See Lindbeck, *Nature of Doctrine*, 122–38 for an exemplary overview of postliberal theology based on a cultural-linguistic frame of reference. Lindbeck notes that it is important to "make a distinction . . . between realistic

historico-critical method simply reaches its categorical limit. In the nature of the case Jesus Christ can be known for who he is only through our response of faith to his own self witness as the risen Savior by means of Word and Spirit.[38]

---

narrative and historical or scientific descriptions. The Bible is often 'history-like' even when it is not 'likely history.' It can therefore be taken seriously in the first respect as a delineator of the character of the divine and human agents, even when its history or science is challenged." 122. Given the nature of the mystery, itself, I see no reason why the revelation of God in Christ cannot come in such a literary form, even as I resonate very much with Packer's biblical hermeneutics, as expressed with such discriminating insight in his collection of essays titled, *Engaging the Written Word of God*. Through such an exploratory hermeneutics, extending from Packer's most subtle grappling with the revelatory mystery of the doctrine of biblical inerrancy to Dorrien's and Lewis's imaginative vision of the inspired Word as true myth, I seek to build on the ongoing dialogue between evangelical (traditional and postconservative) and postliberal discourse on biblical interpretation, theology, and religious culture. It is through such an exploration that I seek to situate critical discussions on the relationship between the Christ of faith and the Jesus of history. From this vantage point, the former serves as the lens for interpreting the significance of the latter in the expectation that God in Christ reconciling the world to himself mediates the difference; a revelation that is now in part, that will later be in full.

38. Hunsinger, "What Can Evangelicals and Postliberals Learn From Each Other?" 144. As argued throughout this book, this is not to deny the reliability and importance of the "historical core" (Fackre, *Doctrine of Revelation*, 20) of the gospel narratives, as so magnificently depicted by Wright. It is to draw permeable boundaries around the limits of historical investigation in detailing the ways in which the revelation of God in Christ reconciling the world to himself bursts forth in the events surrounding the life, ministry, crucifixion, and resurrection sightings of Jesus of Nazareth and his earliest followers. Hunsinger offers an additional insight about both the problematic nature of this claim and the significance of the revelatory mystery in the NT depiction of Jesus of Nazareth as the risen savior of the world; namely:

> That . . . at certain points and to varying degrees, the narratives may actually depict the earthly Jesus in a way that conflates him with the risen Christ, or that superimposes the risen Christ on the earthly Jesus. And yet they may function quite aptly to portray his identity as the narrative intends to convey it. The validity of the narrative portrayal does not necessarily depend on the factuality as narrowly conceived. For the chief "fact" that the narratives wish to convey is precisely that the earthly Jesus and the risen Christ are one and the same. "What Can Evangelicals and Postliberals Learn from Each

The secret things belong to the Lord our God, but the things revealed belong to us and our children forever" (Deut 29:29).

Considered from this angle, the New Testament depiction of Jesus of Nazareth may be viewed by the faith community as "true myth," or if one prefers, true story—even in its most historical-like depictions—one that discloses the radical particularity of the incarnation, both in its veiled and illuminating forms.[39] In terms put by Lewis, "if God chooses to be mythopoeic" through the revelation of the Word of God expressed even in the most historical-like depictions of the gospel narratives, "shall we refuse to be *mythopathic*? For this is the marriage of heaven and earth: perfect myth and perfect fact: claiming not only our love and obedience, but also our wonder and delight,"[40] a perfect union for an incarnational faith. Packer, too, while avoiding the terminology of myth, freely draws upon the centrality of mystery in referring to the revelation of God in human form, whether of Christ or the Bible. As he explains it, "if we can make plain to the church and to the world that our concern in contending for biblical inerrancy is in the first instance soteriological, obediential, doxological, and

---

Other?" 145.

That is, the incarnational revelation of God in Christ reconciling the world can only be grasped through a *theologically rooted* historical insight.

39. I am less concerned whether one draws on the technical language of myth, story, or mystery than in driving home the point that the history-like narratives that shape the gospels throughout, but especially in the post-crucifixion scenes, incorporate all of these aspects, including the historical, which is different than arguing that the gospel narratives are essentially historical, as depicted in the canons of contemporary historiographical description and analysis. Frei emphasizes the gap between the Gnostic myths of savior gods, while Lewis draws on his literary imagination in pointing out the mythological aspects of the gospel narratives. What they share in common is an appreciation of the storied nature of those narratives, even in their most historical-like depictions, which include, history as such, which they both find difficult to disentangle from the their more fictive aspects.

40. Lewis, "Myth Becomes Fact," 42.

devotional—not rationalistic, but religious—we shall do well; if not, we shall do much less well."[41]

As Packer further notes, the entirety of the foundational doctrines of the Great Tradition of Christian orthodoxy are rooted in mystery,[42] including the mystery of the resurrection as well as the sightings. In this he speaks of "*faith-knowledge*: by which we know that God was in Christ reconciling the world to himself." This he identifies as

> a kind of knowledge of which God is both giver and content. It is a Spirit given acquaintance with divine realities, given through acquaintance with God's word. It is a kind of knowledge that makes the knower say in one and the same breath both "whereas I was blind, now I see" (John 9:25 KJV) and also "now we see in a mirror darkly . . . now I know in part" (1 Cor 13:12 ESV). For it is a unique kind of knowledge that, though real, is not full; it is knowledge of what is discernable through a circle of light against a background of a larger darkness; it is, in short, knowledge of a *mystery*, the mystery of the living God at work.[43]
>
> Eye hath not seen, nor ear heard, neither have entered into the heart of man, the things which God hath prepared for them that love him (1 Cor 2:9, KJV).

In all our questing for the historical Jesus, we have learned much while remaining ignorant about a great deal. The likelihood is that some of the most important aspects of the events immediately following the post-crucifixion period may remain simply impenetrable due to the paucity of conclusive evidentiary documentation. Lack of definitive evidence about the reliability of the eye witness testimony is one factor, even as one can—as Wright has, in weighing the various factors—make plausible hypotheses in the construction of a historical research program based on

41. Packer, "The Adequacy of Human Language," 37.
42. Packer, "What Did the Cross Achieve," 58.
43. Ibid., 57.

best case inference analysis.[44] A more complex factor, given the very mystery of the resurrection, is that the confluence of what is commonly referred to as the natural and supernatural forces that were operative, in all likelihood, were more complexly intertwined than we can ever, or are ever called upon, to discern. There may be much wisdom, then, in taking heed that "for now we see only a reflection as in a mirror; then we shall see face to face;" for now we "know in part; then . . . [we] shall know fully, even as . . . [we are] fully known" (1 Cor 13:12). For a faith rooted in the biblical revelation of God in Christ reconciling the world to himself that may be enough. Even so, the historian, the theologian, and the religious seeker have little choice but to press for more.

44. For a contrasting view of Wright's critical realist analysis of the resurrection sightings, see Crossan *Jesus*, 159–92.

Bibliography

Archer, Margaret, et al, eds. *Critical Realism: Essential Readings*. London: Routledge, 1998.

Armstrong, Karen. "Religion: What's God got to do with it?" *New Statesman*. http://www.newstatesman.com/node/164090, 2006.

Bauckham, Richard. *God Crucified: Monotheism and Christology in the New Testament*. Grand Rapids: Eerdmans, 1998.

Bloesch, Donald. *God Almighty: Power, Wisdom, Holiness, Love*. Downers Grove, IL: Intervarsity, 1995.

———. *A Theology of Word and Spirit: Authority and Method in Theology*. Downers Grove, IL: InterVarsity Press, 1992.

Borg, Marcus. J. *Jesus and Buddha: The Parallel Sayings*. Berkeley, CA: Ulysses Press, 1999.

———. *Meeting Jesus Again for the First Time: The Historical Jesus and the Heart of Contemporary Faith*. New York: HarperOne, 1994.

———. *Reading the Bible Again for the First Time*. San Francisco: Harper Collins, 2001.

Borg, Marcus. J., and N. T. Wright. *The Meaning of Jesus: Two Views*. HarperSanFrancisco: San Francisco, 1995.

Clary, Ian. H. "Evangelical Historiography: The Debate over Christian History." *Evangelical Quarterly* 87.3 (2015) 224–51.

Craig, William. L. *Reasonable Faith: Christian Truth and Apologetics*. Third Edition. Wheaton, IL: Crossway, 2008.

Crossan, John Dominic. *The Historical Jesus: The Life of a Mediterranean Jewish Peasant*. New York: HarperCollins, 2010.

———. *Jesus: A Revolutionary Biography*. San Francisco: HarperSanFranciscio, 1994

Demetrion, George. *In Quest of a Vital Protestant Center: An Ecumenical Evangelical Perspective*. Eugene, OR: Wipf and Stock, 2014.

Dorrien, Gary. *The Remaking of Evangelical Theology*. Louisville: Westminster John Knox, 1998.

Evans, C. Stephen. *The Historical Christ and the Jesus of History*. New York: Oxford, 1996.

Fackre, Gabriel. *The Christian Story: Pastoral Systematics*. Vol 1, 3rd ed. *A Narrative Interpretation of Basic Christian Doctrine*. Grand Rapids: Eerdmans, 1996.

———.*The Christian Story: Pastoral Systematics*. Vol 2, *Authority: Scripture in the Church for the World*. Grand Rapids: Eerdmans, 1987.

———. *The Doctrine of Revelation: A Narrative Interpretation*. Grand Rapids: Eerdmans, 1997.

———. *Ecumenical Faith in Evangelical Perspective*. Grand Rapids: Eerdmans, 1993.

Frei, Hans, W. *The Eclipse of Biblical Narrative: A Study in Eighteenth and Nineteenth Hermeneutics*: New Haven: Yale, 1974.

———. *The Identity of Jesus Christ: The Hermeneutical Bases of Dogmatic Theology*. Cascade: Eugene, OR, 2013.

Funk, Robert. W. *The Five Gospels: What Did Jesus Really Say? The Search for the Historical Words of Jesus*. San Francisco: Harper One, 1996.

Grenz, Stanley. J., and John. R. Franke. *Beyond Foundationalism: Shaping Theology in a Postmodern Context*. Louisville: Westminster John Knox, 2001.

Habermas, Jurgen. *Moral Consciousness and Communicative Action*. Cambridge: MIT, 1996.

Hunsinger, George. "What Can Evangelicals and Postliberals Learn from Each Other?" In *The Nature of Confession: Evangelicals and Postliberals in Conversation*, edited by Timothy Phillips and Dennis Okholm, 134–150. Downers Grove, IL: InterVarsity, 1996.

Jeeves, Malcom. *Human Nature and the Millenium. Reflections on the Integration of Psychology and Christianity*. Grand Rapids: Baker, 1997.

Johnson, Phil. "What's Wrong with Wright: Examining the New Perspective on Paul." Ligonier Ministries, http://www.ligonier.org/learn/articles/whats-wrong-wright-examining-new-perspective-paul/. n.d.

Kalas, J. Ellsworth. ed. *Christian Believer: Knowing God with Heart and Mind: Readings*. Nashville: Abingdon, 1999.

———. *Christian Believer: Knowing God with Heart and Mind: Study Manual*. Nashville: Abingdon, 1999.

Lewis, C. S. *Mere Christianity*. New York: HarperCollins, 2001.

———. "Myth Became Fact." In Lewis, *The Grand Miracle and Other Selected Essays in Theology and Ethics from God in the Dock*, 38–42. New York: Ballantine, 1970.

Lindbeck, George A. *The Nature of Doctrine: Religion and Theology in Postliberal America*. Louisville: Westminster John Knox.

Long, V. Philips. *The Art of Biblical History*. Grand Rapids: Zondervan, 1994.

Marsden, George. *The Soul of the Modern University*. New York: Oxford, 1994.

Moltmann, Jurgen. *The Way of Jesus Christ: Christology in Messianic Dimensions*. Minneapolis: Fortress, 1993.

Newbigin, Lesslie. *Foolishness to the Greeks: The Gospel and Western Culture*. Grand Rapids: Eerdmans, 1986.

———. *The Gospel in a Pluralistic Society*. Grand Rapids: Eerdmans, 1989.

Niebuhr, H. Richard. "The Center of Value." In *Radical Monotheism and Western Culture: With Supplementary Essays*, 100–13. Louisville: Westminster/John Knox, 1960.

Olson, Roger E. *The Journey of Modern Theology: From Reconstruction to Deconstruction*. Downers Grove, IL: Intervarsity Press, 2013.

Packer, J. I. "The Adequacy of Human Language." In *Engaging the Written Word of God*, 19–42. Peabody, MA: Henderson, 1999.

———. *Engaging the Written Word of God*. Peabody, MA: Henderson, 1999.

———. *Knowing and Doing the Will of God: Daily Devotions for Every Day of the Year*. New York: Testament Books 2000.

———. *Knowing God*. Downers Grove, IL: Intervarsity, 1993.

———. "Understanding the Bible: Evangelical Hermenutics." In *Engaging the Written Word of God*, 137–49. Peabody, MA: Henderson, 1999.

———. "What Did the Cross Achieve? The Logic of Penal Substitution." In *In My Place Condemned He Stood: Celebrating the Glory of the Atonement*, edited by J. I. Packer and Mark Dever, 53-100. Wheaton, IL: Crossway, 2007.

Phillips, Timothy R., and Dennis L. Okhlom, eds. *The Nature of Confession: Evangelicals and Postliberals in Conversation*. Downers Grove, IL: InterVarsity, 1993.

Pinnock, Clark H. *Biblical Revelation: The Foundation of Christian Theology, 1971*. Chicago: Moody.

Piper, John. *The Future of Justification: A Response to N. T. Wright*. Wheaton: Crossway, 2007.

Purdue, Leo C. *The Collapse of History: Reconstructing Old Testament Theology*. Minneapolis: Fortress, 1994.

Sherman, Steven. B. *Revitalizing Theological Epistemology: Holistic Evangelical Approaches to the Knowledge of God*. Eugene, OR: Pickwick, 2008.

Stein, Robert H. "N. T. Wright's *Jesus and the Victory of God*: A Review Essay." *Journal of Evangelical Theology Society* 44:2 (2001) 207–18.

Taylor, Charles. *A Secular Age*. Cambridge: Belknap Press of Harvard University Press, 2007.

Wright, N. T. *The Contemporary Quest for Jesus*. Minneapolis: Fortress, 2002.

———. *Christian Origins and the Question of God*. Vol. 1. *The New Testament and the People of God*. Minneapolis: Fortress, 1992.

———. *Christian Origins and the Question of God*. Vol. 2. *Jesus and the Victory of God*. Minneapolis: Fortress, 1996.

———. *Christian Origins and the Question of God*. Vol. 3. *The Resurrection of the Son of God*. Minneapolis: Fortress, 2003.

———. *Simply Christian: Why Christianity Makes Sense*. San Francisco: HarperSanFrancisco, 2006.

Yong, Amos. *The Dialogical Spirit: Christian Reason and Theological Method in the Third Millennium*. Eugene, OR: Cascade, 2014.

Author Index

Subject Index

Scripture Index